Terra & Nodia, may the blessings
of the Great Spirit bless your
healing journey,

the *the* MAKING *of a* HEALER

Russell Jous Eagles

the MAKING
of a HEALER

TEACHINGS OF MY ONEIDA GRANDMOTHER

RUSSELL FOUREAGLES

This publication has been generously supported by
The Kern Foundation

QUEST
BOOKS

Theosophical Publishing House
Wheaton, Illinois * Chennai, India

Quest Books
Theosophical Publishing House
PO Box 270
Wheaton, IL 60187-0270

www.questbooks.net

Cover photo by Katie Wilder
Frontispiece photo (Russel FourEagles and client) by Todd Dacquisto
Cover design by Drew Stevens
Typesetting by Wordstop, Chennai, India

Library of Congress Cataloging-in-Publication Data

FourEagles, Russell.
   The making of a healer: teachings of my Oneida grandmother / Russell FourEagles.—First Quest edition.
        pages   cm
Includes index.
ISBN 978-0-8356-0927-2
1. FourEagles, Russell, 1951—. 2. Oneida Indians—Biography.
3. Shamans—Wisconsin—Biography. 4. Grandmothers—Wisconsin—Biography. 5. Grandparent and child—Wisconsin. 6. Oneida Indians—Medicine. 7. Healing. 8. Oneida Indians—Social life and customs.
9. Vietnam War, 1961–1975—Veterans—United States—Biography.
10. Post-traumatic stress disorder—Treatment. I. Title.
E99.O45F68 2014
305.897'5543092-dc23
[B]   2014026040

5   4   3   *   15   16   17   18   19   20

Printed in the United States of America

Table of Contents

TABLE OF CONTENTS

Russell FourEagles, 1971

Russell and Gram

Preface

This book recounts the lessons I learned as a child from my maternal grandmother, Coretta Mae Smith, who was a healer in the Oneida Tribe tradition, the Oneidas being part of the Iroquois Confederation. The teachings she passed on to me have been passed down unbroken, as she put it, for "two hundred generations of grandmothers." But I now know that I am the 202nd grandchild medicine person in my family (and the seventh *male* healer), which would make 404 generations altogether; so I think the lineage goes back much further than my grandmother realized. A "generation" being twenty years, the healing techniques I learned from Gram are somewhere around eight thousand years old. Now I pass them on to you so that they can continue to help people.

I have been filling notebooks with the information in this book for a very long time. But I first got the idea for writing it after a healing I did for my friend Bob. He had had a stroke while driving and was in very bad shape when I visited him in the hospital. The doctor told Tom, Bob's brother, that Bob would never walk or talk or even feed himself again. He said Tom had better see about finding a nursing home for Bob, as the medical staff could do very little for him; he had lain in the car too long to dissolve the clot that caused the stroke.

Bob is a large man, six feet four inches tall, and weighs nearly four hundred pounds. When I had a chance, I asked his doctor if it was okay for me to work on his patient. He said, "As it happens, I am Lakota, and so I do know something about healers. But I don't know much, because my training is in Western medicine." I told him that the Creator can do anything; and he, being of Native American descent himself, thought my healing work was a good thing.

I began a healing for Bob. First I found the clot and had the Creator dissolve it. After a couple of minutes, Bob started to get feeling back in his hand, and I said, "You should be able to move your fingers." And he did. Soon he was able to move his arm and various other parts of his body, as I worked to fix the connections in different spots in his brain.

In a healthy brain, the connections between cells are spaced a certain distance apart to keep the charge of electricity constant from cell to cell; this current doesn't diminish whether we are accessing memories or absorbing new information. But then, let's say, a person has a stroke, which happens when a blood clot blocks an artery supplying blood to the brain. At the point where the clot creates a dam, the part of the brain that is blocked becomes starved of blood, causing the matter that holds the brain cells in place there to shrink. The connections between the cells in that area get too close together and can't fire properly to transmit signals. At the same time, in the part of the brain in front of the clot, the brain matter swells. The distance between the connections widens, which also makes the signals misfire.

I said, "You can move your leg now." And Bob kicked his covers right off the bed, mumbling something at me. The doctor sat there wide eyed, not knowing what to think. "That was like nothing I've ever seen before!" he said. "Even though I know about healers because I came from the reservation, I never saw anything like that."

As it turned out, Bob was in the hospital only a short amount of time—I think it was three days—before he was home and walking again. I told him to get out of the hospital quickly, because it is a place for sick people and he was definitely not sick.

I visited him regularly at home, and he started asking questions about what it is that I do. I told him that I channel the Creator and that it is the Creator who does the healing. "The Creator will do much of the work," I told him, "but it takes the person being healed to finish the job." In other words, the Creator does half the healing and we have to earn the other half.

Bob said to me, "This stuff is amazing. You should write a book." I thought about it for a long time and decided to give it a try. I know nothing of writing or how to do it. I can't spell for sour beans, but with the help of spell checker and some of the friends I have made over the years, as you see, the book got done.

In all ways, this is a true story, even though some of the names have been changed to protect the innocent and to keep ten thousand cousins off my back. Any resemblance to people, places, or things, other than those clearly intended, is purely coincidental. None of the herbs I discuss here should be used without the guidance of a licensed herbalist. Nothing I say is meant to replace modern medicine. Always check with your doctor to see if use of any healing technique is permitted.

Acknowledgments

I thank my grandmother, Coretta Mae Smith, for setting me on this journey and guiding me throughout it. I also thank my awesome wife, Shelly, for dealing with the countless hours I have spent with my head stuck in the computer as I transcribed my handwritten notebooks; my children Shayne, Tonya, Travis, Ashley, and Siara for accepting my not being able to be there for them as much as I would have liked; and all my other mentors through the years. Finally, I thank my outstanding agent, Rebecca Schaller, for seeing what could be; and my editor, Sharron Dorr, for turning my native-speak into something wonderfully understandable and readable.

My Heritage

In 1870, my great-grandfather Henry Peaceful Lake (Smith) was living in a wigwam on the Rainy River in Ontario, near where the Little Canoe River dumped into the Rainy. This was before the dam was completed in 1905 and the impoundment became known as Rainy Lake. Henry's father was Ojibwa, with a bit of French blood, and his mother was Oneida, from the Six-Nations' area of Canada.

Around 1867 or 1868, the Canadian government passed a law stating that all Indians were to be moved to reservations and to cease their native traditions. The Royal Canadian Mounted Police (RCMP) came to Henry's lodge and told him that he must move to the reserve called Couchiching. When he asked why, they said that the government had made a treaty with the Indians on the other side of the river and that Henry's lodge was now on Crown land.

"But those are not my people across the river, and this is not their land to sell," said Henry. "My father, his father before him, and many grandfathers before them have lived here. My people are buried here. I can't sell you the bones of my ancestors. Up and down the river, as far as you see, this is my land. It was passed to me by my father. So I am not moving."

"Oh, yes you are," said the police as they pulled their guns on Henry.

"What about my traps, my guns, and my other possessions?"

"Leave them," they replied. "Everything you need will be provided at Couchiching."

"Right," my great-grandfather scoffed, not knowing how perceptive he truly was.

This story I learned from my grandmother, as my great-grandfather had died before I could meet him. She also told me that on the way to Couchiching, which was a sixty-five-mile journey, Henry got the brilliant idea that if the Crown could buy land from someone who didn't own it, then maybe there was a chance that he, too, could make some money off the Crown. He asked if the Royal Canadian Mounted Police wanted to buy a lot of land, really cheap. The police inquired as to what he had to sell. He offered them Minnesota for $50,000. "And that *would* be cheap," he added.

The police said that he couldn't sell Minnesota because he didn't own it and that, it being in the United States of America, they had no authority there, to which my great-grandfather responded, "But I *do* own my land, and that didn't stop you from taking *it*."

Their only reaction was, "Give us a break; we're just doing our job."

After they finally reached the Couchiching Reserve, the police told Henry to sit on a bench outside the agent's office and not move while they went inside to fill out his paperwork. However, my great-grandfather had other things in mind. He ran down the hill to the Rainy River, jumped into a birch-bark canoe, and paddled across the river to International Falls, Minnesota. When the Mounties saw him crossing the river, they ran down to the bank and shouted that he had to come back.

"You have no authority here, remember?" Henry yelled over his shoulder. "This is the United States of America!"

So the police had to return to the agent's office and report the loss of a wild Indian. Great-grandfather immigrated into the United States stating, "I am a free man and don't have to live on any reservation."

When Henry crossed the border in 1870, the US immigration officials tried to spell his native name three times, each time crossing it out. They eventually made him an American by giving him the name *Smith*. With the help of my local library, I was able to locate his immigration papers from 1870 on a micro disc, which is how I became aware of this interesting fact. (The native name as it appears on the micro disc is nearly illegible. As close as my cousins could translate it, it means "Peaceful Lake.")

Over the next year, my great-grandfather traveled the trails of northern Minnesota, always going southeast. He maintained that he was a free man, but eventually he moved to within a quarter of a mile or so of a reservation. It's my understanding that, by 1871, he ended up near the Oneida Reservation at Oconto, Wisconsin, renting a house directly across the street from it. There, he met and married Birdie Hoover.

Birdie was a great-granddaughter of Chief Neopit, the last hereditary chief of the Menominee before they lost their independence and were moved to a reservation. Chief Neopit (Four in Den) later became a judge in the reserve court system. Birdie was of Oneida and Menominee descent and reportedly a cousin of a famous FBI man who didn't claim his native heritage. Birdie stood five feet six in height, which was tall for an Oneida woman. She was of slight build and had icy blue eyes like those of her mother and grandmother.

Coretta Mae Smith, my gram, was born to Henry and Birdie in 1889. Like her mother, Coretta was rather tall for an Oneida woman. She, too, had icy blue eyes, was of slight build, and was very strong. Her daughter, Lauretta, would eventually marry my father, Edward FourEagles.

My father's parents were Charles and Minerva (Scar) FourEagles. Charles, who was born in Pennsylvania in 1870, was of mostly German descent but carried an Indian last name from his father, who was half German. Charles stood six feet ten inches tall. My paternal grandmother, Minerva, who was predominantly Ojibwa with also some German and Dakota, was four feet six.

My mother, Lauretta, was born in 1922. She was five feet two in height with a background on her mother's side of Menominee Ojibwa and Oneida and on her father's side of Norwegian. Her father died in Milwaukee, one of the first people to be hit and killed by a horseless carriage, or, as he called them, "those infernal noisy things." I believe that happened about thirty years before I was born.

Gram and I

To my parents, Lauretta and Edward FourEagles, I was born in my grandmother's house in 1951 near a small town in northwestern Wisconsin called Trego. I had many brothers and sisters: Vernon and Helen died before I was born; and Roy, Gerald, and Geraldine were born after me. At the time of my birth, that left just my older siblings, Edward and Virginia, and me to reside with our parents in our twelve-by-fourteen-foot tarpaper shack. It had a partial slab-wood floor, a wood-burning stove, and kerosene lamps hanging from the ceiling. We had no television set, radio, or even electricity until 1959. Then my father and the neighbors cleared a swath of forest so that the electric company could put up their poles.

The year my brother Roy was born, my mother asked Gram if one of us kids could live with her because there wasn't enough room in our house, and Gram chose me. I told my mother that I didn't want to go live with an old Indian woman. Mom said, "It will be okay because she is your grandmother."

Gram's and my life was majestic in its simplicity. We left the table feeling satisfied, but no food was ever wasted. We had no television or radio. Instead, Gram would tell me legends of the people. She would ask me so many questions that I would end up telling her more stories, many times over, than she would tell me. If I made a mistake, she had me repeat the correct version until I got it right. "You need to remember these things," she would say, "as you might someday be the only one with this knowledge."

Gram became very special to me, and I to her. She once told me that I was the first "Indigo" baby she had ever seen. I believe my being Indigo must have excited her because of all the wisdom and lessons she planned to pass on to me. Children known as "Indigo" have been born since the 1950s, although there couldn't have been many at that time if I was the first one my gram saw. Indigo children feel more with their hearts and are not so preoccupied with the greed that seems to have taken over our society. Fortunately, some of these young people will be the upcoming politicos, doctors, and other people of power in this country.

Today, Indigos are often diagnosed as people with attention deficit disorder. The trouble with them is that they learn really fast and get bored quickly, because, in most cases, they have already gotten the point and stored it away. They can pick up information just by being around it. I never took a book home all the time I was in school, but my grades were good enough to allow me to study herbs with Gram on weekends. Indigo children have an inner knowing, so it is hard to deceive them. If you tell an Indigo child that you're going to do something, you had better do it, because if you don't, that person will remember it throughout life. At any rate, I still do. And you need to be honest with Indigos, as they will be with you. They may seem somewhat temperamental, but in reality they are just being honest, even if they sometimes seem totally in your face. Usually, though, people refuse to listen to them with open ears that hear.

After I started school, I lived with my parents during the week and lived with Gram only on weekends and during the summers. When I was with her I studied herbs and whatnot, and Gram spent a lot of time doing healings. Occasionally, a client would stop by her house, but most often someone would take us to the client. The healings could last up to three days. During these sessions there would be dancers and drummers, and there was always lots of excitement. How Gram made all the arrangements without phones and electricity was beyond me.

After telephones came into the area, Gram used her phone to call people in for either singing or chanting, depending on the type of healing it was. Much later, when I started doing healings on my own, I figured out that the drummers and dancers were used to distract clients, thus making it easier for the clients to stay out of their own way.

My own technique for getting clients to stay out of their own way is simply to keep them engaged in light conversation. That way, I find that they become more relaxed and less focused on what I am doing, which allows them to be more receptive to the healing. Laughter is another way I help people relax. The old saying that laughter is the best medicine is still true.

Gram continued to do healings throughout my childhood as I dutifully watched, listened, and learned. At such a young age, I was unaware of how great an impact these lessons would someday have on me. It is funny how they come back time and again when they are needed.

The old ways are good and right, but whatever the way, it is all in the Creator's plan. I am grateful that it was within the Creator's plan for me to live off the reservation when I was growing up. That way, not having to attend the reservation schools, I was free to learn lessons in the old ways from Gram.

A Village Teaches

One day, as Gram and I harvested red clover blossoms in the field behind her house, I, as usual, was listening to her tell stories. This was one of the times when she was talking of the things *her* grandmother had told her.

"In my grandmother's village," Gram said, "no one went without. If a woman's man got killed, someone in the village would usually marry her. If no one was available, usually a brother of the deceased would marry her, even if he was already married. The women would then become sisters and sister-wives. That way, everyone was taken care of, and no one was left behind."

Gram went on to say that, in her grandmother's village, when it came time to teach the young ones the parents weren't the ones who did it. Instead, the aunts, uncles, grandmas, and grandpas taught them and did the disciplining. The parents' job, in contrast, was just to love their kids. And things were much better in those days. The kids would run to their parents if they got in trouble, rather than away from them as they do today. Children running from parents is simply a reaction to parents having become the disciplinarians and to the kids not having any contact—or not as much as they should— with grandparents, aunts, and uncles.

I may have been a bit young to understand these things, as Gram was talking about them in 1955 or 1956, when I was about five. But she continued, "Now there are kids who call themselves *beatniks*. You wouldn't have found that in my grandmother's day. Ever since we began this new system of teaching kids outside the home, society has been going downhill; people don't have much respect for elders. Be sure you always honor the elders, because if it weren't for them, you wouldn't be here. We give freely to the young people; all you have to do is listen."

I can't imagine what Gram's response would be about something I recently saw on the news. In a poll taken in a big city out west, high school kids were asked where food comes from. To my disbelief, 30 to 40 percent of them answered, "the store!" I realize that not every grandma was like mine, but where have our values gone? How is it possible that so many of our children are not taught about the real things anymore? Eating is a basic necessity for survival. Yet those high school kids knew nothing about the origin of their food. In contrast, I know for a fact that I would never have starved if something horrific had happened. And the last place I'd have looked for food would have been the store.

Who is actually teaching our children? It seems that parents look to the schools, and the schools look to the parents. Sadly enough, the kids are not looking anywhere.

Also sad is that, unlike in Gram's day, now the responsibility for child-rearing is left entirely to just the two parents increasingly isolated from other family members. We love our children. Yet society as a whole has taught us to pass the buck. We send the children to school or a babysitter, while we go make money. The parents have to work in order to provide for their families. This in itself is acceptable. The problem is that, in most households, now *both* parents are working, because it takes two incomes just to survive.

Unfortunately, we work more and more, wanting more and more things to store in the garage so that we can pull them out once a year for vacationing. We notice our neighbors' fancy cars, and all of a sudden ours isn't good enough. "We must make more money," we tell ourselves, which usually means that we work even more.

Children don't get out to the parks or woods anymore, which is another sad thing. Instead, they are fully occupied with the expensive clothes, computers, and cell phones to which they are accustomed. So again, we work more.

Meanwhile, life becomes so hectic that we forget about our own parents and grandparents. Elders are put into nursing homes, left to be forgotten. Unfortunately, the love, wisdom, experiences, and presence of those relatives are also forgotten.

So, without having to care for our elders, we have even more time to acquire money. But that "gain" is actually a pity, considering how harmful it is to today's family. And even then, we *still* have trouble making enough money.

What we must remember is what we've forgotten: it's all about the children. The native nations valued their children above all else. But now, the *children* are the ones who are losing. They are losing out on the time that we—their parents, their grandparents, or any other adult relative—could be giving them. I truly believe that there are very few parents or grandparents who would turn their backs if their child had a question or a problem to solve, but we are not available, for we are out working (unless we're already in a nursing home). The family unit has transformed itself into little more than strangers living under the same roof. Working is pretty much unavoidable in today's society. But balance and clarity about our priorities is what we need to strive for. It isn't easy, but we have to try.

Society has taught us to buy the children things, because that's what they want. Simply stated, what children *need* is their families.

But society wants to keep the corporate machine well oiled and running smoothly; and, of course, that's what the corporations want, too: let's make a new holiday so that we can sell, sell, sell and buy, buy, buy.

Sadly, we are not doing for our children today what Gram did for me. As I've said, when a child I was lucky to live off the reservation, so I never had the Indian beat out of me as so many of my cousins did. At the same time, I am sad not to have had the closeness with my people that my gram had. (Even though she and her parents didn't live on the Oneida Reservation, they did live across the street from it, and she had plenty of contact with that community.) I'm glad I grew up with her beliefs, for a day doesn't go by without a memory, a lesson, or Gram's pure love present in my mind and heart. This is why I am able to pass the old teachings on to my clients.

And I wonder: if, as Gram taught, we are supposed to make decisions based on what will benefit not only our grandchildren but the next seven generations to come—and the children of today are already losing—what does that say for the next seven generations?

How the Medicine Came to the Clan of My Grandmother

Here is the story as Gram told it to me: Long ago in a far, distant time and place, an old man came upon an Iroquois village. The old man was poorly dressed and looked tired and hungry. As he walked through the village, he looked at the doors of the long houses. Over each door was the symbol of the clan that lived within.

Above the door of the first lodge was the Turtle Clan emblem in the form of a huge turtle shell. Poking his head into the blanketed door, the old man asked for food and shelter against the night. But his request fell upon deaf ears, and the woman of the house said, "Go away, you ugly old man. Move on out of here."

The next long house he saw had a stuffed snipe over its door. Again, when he asked for help, the woman of the lodge told him to go on his way. "Please leave us alone and bother someone else. Now git," she said.

From clan to clan he went, looking for food and a place to lie down for the night. The Wolf, Beaver, Deer, Eel, Heron, and Eagle Clans all turned him away, not wanting anything to do with him. "Ragged old man," they said as he moved through the village.

Nearing the end of the village, the old man despaired as his hunger and weariness grew. He decided to try one last time at the last little home, which had a carved bear's head above the door. An old woman of the Bear Clan came out of the house. She took pity on the stranger. She saw how tired the old man was and invited him inside to share whatever she had, meager though it was. The old woman was a gracious host. She gave the man her only food and a deer skin upon which to rest for the night, with a rolled robe for a pillow.

The old man awoke the next day ill with a fever. He told the old woman to go into the forest and find a particular plant. When she returned with it, the old man taught her how to make the plant into a medicine tea. Drinking it, the old man was cured. Because the old woman was so good to him, he asked to stay with her for a few days. Several times during his stay, he became ill again. Each time it was a different type of malady, and each time he sent the old woman into the forest for a different herb. The old man instructed the woman on the proper preparation of the herbs to cure each particular ailment. When he drank the medicine, his condition improved.

One day the woman returned home and saw a bright light coming from within. Approaching the door, she came face to face with a handsome young man whose face shone like the sun. The old woman was frightened, believing a spirit stood in her way.

But the young man calmed the woman, saying, "Do not be afraid. I am the Creator of all things. I came to the lodges of the Iroquois as an old man so that I could see who would help me. At each clan's lodge, I asked for food and shelter and was turned away. You, good woman of the Bear Clan, were the only one to offer me assistance. Because you showed me compassion, I have taught you cures for all the illnesses that afflict the real people.

"The people who seek your advice need to bring you tobacco; that way I'll know they come with a good mind, and I can help you when you use their tobacco in prayers for whatever they need. Understand that the tobacco is not a payment but an offering. Their payment for healing should be trade goods of some sort—anything you need, because you will be too busy to make them yourself."

Destined to Heal

Gram and I did a lot of talking around her little blonde oak table in what I would call her breakfast nook. It wasn't really a nook;

it was just a table by a window where we could look and see what was going on in the outside world.

One day when I was five years old, Gram told me that her mother, her grandmother, and more than two hundred generations of grandmothers back in time had been healers. It seemed she recited names of ancestors for more than an hour. Then she said that I was to be the next healer. However, I would have to stay out of the Creator's way.

"All those people, Grandma, are women," I said, thinking that she had missed the obvious. "And I am a man."

She replied, "There were some grandfathers, too, who were medicine people. Besides, you *will* be a man, but right now you're a little boy; you are just *male*. And it is okay that you are male because you are the one with the Creator's gift, the gift of healing with your hands."

"Is the Creator going to chase me down if I don't stay out of his way?" I asked.

Gram just laughed. Because I was a young child, I didn't realize that "staying out of the way" meant allowing the power of the Creator to work through me. I was not sure what to make of my grandma's belief that I was to become a healer, so I didn't give it much thought. Often, though, when little birds broke their necks flying into my folks' windows, I felt compelled to help them. I would pick an injured bird up, hold it for a few minutes, and ask the Creator God to take care of it. It would then fly away. At that age, I didn't think of it as healing; I only thought of it as the Creator taking care of the little birds. This was actually an early and direct experience of the Creator's power.

Although a good forty-five years may have passed since I started to do healings, there are some things the Creator never lets me forget, including the bird healings of my childhood and how the energy felt while working on those and other little critters.

When I was a child, Gram explained, "The people who do healing are chosen by the Creator. We are just like a buffalo horn, a hollow vessel to transmit the love [energy] that the Creator sends us. He transmits love to everyone, but most people are not capable of receiving it or not able to understand what is being given to them. Usually, they don't believe. In essence, people are in their own way. They perceive the love transmitted to them as random thoughts that make no sense."

As a five-year-old, I asked, "Will that happen to me?"

Grandma responded, "No, you are a healer. The length of time it takes you to understand this is up to you. The Creator gives us the free will to act or not to act on what he tells us. At first, you, like most people, might not believe; but because you are a healer, you will eventually."

"I don't think I will ever be able to do that. Are you sure I'm going to be a healer man?"

"Yes, my boy, even though it will be a while before you become one. Just be careful what you send to the universe."

Over and Over

Once Gram and I were sitting at her table as she cleaned purple flowers. I watched to make sure I could do it right when I was a bit bigger, and as I watched we talked.

"Russell, do you know why I have you repeat these things that I teach you, over and over?"

"Because I need to know them—right, Gram?" I responded.

She replied, "Yes, that's part of it. Just know that I am not doing it to be mean or disrespectful. If I don't get you to remember these things correctly, then they will be lost. And if they get lost, they will be gone forever. And what would that mean?"

"I guess that no one else would be able to hear them?"

"Yes, that's it. So just remember that the only reason I have you do this is so that, sometime in the future, you will be able to tell your own children and others the stories exactly as I learned them from my own mother and grandmother."

"Gram, this seems like a big load to hand to a ten-year-old," I said.

"Don't worry, you won't always be ten. You will be learning this stuff for many years to come. Eventually, you will be able to recite it in your sleep."

Oh, great, I thought to myself, not daring to say so out loud.

Gram went on to explain, "In the old days after a healing, people brought food, horses, tanned leather, and all manner of things. It's only since I was a girl that money has come into play, because paying with it is easier than tanning hides or catching a horse. People always brought tobacco as an offering, and some people nowadays think of *it* as a payment. But remember what the Creator said to the old woman in the story of how medicine came to my clan: Tobacco should in no way be considered payment for a healing. Instead, it is brought so that the healer can use it in prayers for the client.

"Bringing tobacco is just the proper thing to do with any elder when you want to talk to them about something. It doesn't have to be about healing. But if you need advice—if you have a question—that is how we do it. And with healings, tobacco should always be used as an offering and not as a payment. Remember that, Russell."

Revelations of a Dream

Ever since I was six years old, I have heard of a prophecy proclaiming a worldwide disaster that will take place in the twenty-first century. My Oneida grandmother told me what her grandmother had told her: that the day would come when Mother Earth would become tired of our trespasses against her. It was said that when people had quit taking care of the earth for long enough, Mother Earth would rebel. A global cleansing would occur, meaning a reversal of the poles when everything gets swept away except for a vestige of people to start over.

"How will I know when these things are going to happen?" I asked my grandmother.

She replied, "When it doesn't get to be twenty below zero in Spooner, Wisconsin, anymore and we don't get eight feet of snow, you'll know it is coming. You will notice strange things, such as birds migrating north in the fall."

In the fall of 2009, my clients and I saw a flock of geese flying south, as usual, but with a V that was pointing east. That could be a sign that the magnetic grid is changing, interfering with the geese's sense of direction. We also saw many geese that were flying in the shape of one-sided Vs. Several clients told me they saw the same thing in different parts of the country.

My gram said there would be other signs, too, beginning with changes in the weather. The sun would start to emit small particles that would make people more tired with less work.

"You'll sunburn more easily, and you will feel older than you are," she told me. "The Creator in his infinite wisdom has made things to work one way when we take care of them and another when we don't. If we take care of Mother Earth, she works for us; if we don't, she works against us. Both ways are perfectly right for each situation. Remember, the Creator not only gave us free will, he also gave it to his child, Mother Earth."

Gram said that a lot of people would be going away because they no longer cared about the Earth Mother. I asked if everyone would have to die; at six years of age, I was worried by the idea of death.

She said, "No, just be sure always to help the Earth Mother, because she will save the people who care for her so that they can repopulate the earth. The Creator will see to it."

She went on to say that this would not be the first time Mother Earth will have done a cleansing. It has happened three times in the past: the first two were millions of years ago and Noah's flood was the last one. (To those who say that people haven't been around for millions of years, I can only answer that, according to Gram, our people walked with the giant lizards and that once, now lost in time, there were great cities with advanced technology just as there are today.)

"I think the fourth cleansing—the one coming—will be the last," she said. "The Creator made this place for the people to live, and it was good. But eventually, people forget where everything comes from. They make religion a business and, when they do bad things, they blame a fictitious being. Instead of taking responsibility for their own actions, the way the Oneida people do, they say the devil made them do it. Even some of our own people have taken up the way of the Europeans and lost their way."

Gram explained that the great cleansing would commence on December 12, 2012. The predicted polar shift would be in full force ten days later, or by December 21, 2012, with the Mayan long-count calendar finally ending on that day.

When she mentioned 2012, I said, "Gram, that year will never be here." She told me that even though by then I would have grandchildren, assuredly that year would come. Nevertheless, to a young child in 1955, the year 2012 seemed forever into the future.

On June 13, 2003, I awoke from a dream in which I saw the worldwide electric grid had been knocked out by an electromagnetic spike from the sun or from somewhere else in space. People were perishing as gas and food supplies dwindled. Vehicles were abandoned all over Highway 53. People were fighting over slight morsels of food. My wife and children and I, however, had prepared for this. We were bunked up and equipped with a garden.

The dream left me feeling very uneasy, as I realized that the stories Gram had told me might have been more than mere *Indian* legends. Furthermore, scientists had begun seeing signs that the poles are weakening, which in turn is a sign of massive global changes. I am not a fatalist, and I am not even afraid. But, after putting all of Gram's clues and information together, I am cautious. These global changes could have devastating repercussions worldwide.

Reading forecasts of possible drought and famine added to my uneasiness. And things are coming to pass as Gram said they would: it has been hotter and dryer than it has ever been, and the water tables are dropping, which is noticeable here in Wisconsin, where you can now see lakes with fifteen or twenty extra feet of beach. When I moved to my healing center, Soaring Eagles Wellness, the little pond on the property was one acre in size; now it is only about twenty feet across, just a shadow of its former self.

The signs are here for anyone interested enough to read them. So please, open your eyes and look around. More and more of my clients are seeing the changes but are unsure of what they mean.

They just know that something is definitely wrong. They feel it in the weather and in the air. The more open you are, and the more you get out of your own way, the easier it is to see. Being in your own way is like being in a box and not wanting to leave; it gives you a very narrow perspective. Get out of your own way and start observing! Seeing is believing, believing is knowing, and knowing is wisdom.

Gram passed on many years before the Mayan calendar ended, but I recently had a communication about it with her in a vision. I was worried that I wouldn't have time to complete all my projects before the cleansing arrives. She said I was worrying needlessly. While she was alive she thought our present-day Western calendar was right; but, now that she has passed, she sees that it and the time-keeping method of her people are two different things. Our modern calendar is off by a good number of years, and the cleansing she spoke of is still far in the future; it might not even take place in my lifetime.

"What about all the talk of 2012, then?" I asked.

"Don't worry your sweet head; just let them talk. It's the prattle of idle minds."

The Creation Story

One evening Gram and I were on the couch looking at the multitude of stars that shone down on us. "You know where all those stars come from?" Gram asked me.

"I don't," I said. This was when I first heard the creation story from my grandmother, which is the version told in the Bear Clan:

In the beginning there was nothing—a complete void. There was no light, no dark, only the Creator. For eons the Creator stood within the void thinking, what will I do? I would like to have children and places for them to live, food for them to eat, and whatever else they need.

With a great clap of his hands came a compression that caused the loudest boom ever *not* heard—for, of course, no one was there to hear it. Out of the clap came sound and light. The universe was born, and billions and trillions of stars formed. From the leftover dust and energy, the Creator began making innumerable worlds around many of the suns, including the earth. He was getting ready for the coming of his children.

The Creator seeded life in the water and waited eagerly for its growth. One of his days would seem like an eternity for us. He watched and he waited, and he waited and watched. Eventually, the seeds of life took hold, and the grasses, flowers, and animals grew and populated the many worlds he seeded. When the time was right on each world, he created first man and first woman. Starting far to the east of our world, he seeded the first humans and went from world to world until he was far west of us. The beings that live in the worlds east of the earth are our elder and wiser brothers and sisters. Those people who live to the west of us are younger than we are and less evolved, so to speak.

When the time was right for our world, the Creator made the first man and first woman here. He scooped up red dust by Lake Superior and formed a man, giving him the energy from the right side of the Creator's body. Then the Creator scooped more dust and made a woman, giving her the energy from the left side of his body. (We now call this energy DNA.)

The Creator spent his time watching his children grow—not just the two-legged ones, but all his children, from the smallest to the largest—never interfering, just watching. Then he said, "This is good."

Because it was cold at night, he gave the early humans fur. He watched and saw that they were having trouble surviving. This was because they had no fire to warm themselves and barely enough skill to feed themselves, even with all the food he gave to them.

The Creator tried again. He scooped up more dust and made another man and woman. This time, he made them smarter and gave them the ability to make skin clothes, because he had not given them as much fur on their bodies. These people were doing better, but they did not acknowledge their Father.

Thousands of years later, they had still not acknowledged their Father, and so the Creator tried again. This time he went again to the south shore of Lake Superior and got two more piles of red dust. He then went to the white cliffs of Dover in England and grabbed two handfuls of white dust and set them next to the red dust. Then he brought back two piles of yellow dust from the Gobi Desert and, finally, two piles of black dust from the shores of Africa.

For each pair of piles, he gave energy from one half his body to one pile and energy from the other half of his body to the other pile. And so we have the four basic races of humankind—red, white, yellow, and black.

Those colors are also the colors of our medicine wheel. If you ask most Indians with a boarding-school background why, they will say the colors are for the sacred directions. And that is partially true. But, originally, the colors were in honor of our brothers and sisters of different races whom—after various scatterings over the earth—we wouldn't see again for maybe hundreds of thousands of years.

This Land Is Our Land

Gram and I were taking a walk as she talked of what her grandmother had told her about how America was discovered. She explained that our land was ours because we, the Oneida, had fought with the Americans against the British to help win the Revolutionary War.

She said, "The Oneida and the Tuscarora were the only tribes in the Iroquois confederation that did not remain neutral. We fought with the revolutionary soldiers against the British to free America from the Crown's overbearing control. And so, after the revolution, the new President Washington said that our land around Lake Oneida in New York would be ours for as long as the grass shall grow and the rivers will flow. That sounded good at the time, but we didn't know the rivers were going to dry up so quickly.

"Around the 1820s or '30s, the US government forced the Turtle and Wolf Clans of the Oneida people to move to the wilds of Canada or Wisconsin, giving them part of the Menominee Reserve in northeast Wisconsin. A lot of the Bear Clan stayed in Canada or on the tiny piece of New York that we had left.

"They gave us, and almost all the other native people, reservations. There were several native tribes that didn't war with the United States (or if they did, they never made a treaty with the government). As a result, the government does not recognize them as a tribe of people, as if they came from someplace else—Venus, maybe? Then the government kept picking off little pieces of the reservations, until out of the millions of square miles that the people owned, all we had left were a few small spots of land.

"I believe that of the six to seven hundred nations that were here when Columbus arrived, the languages were derived from thirteen or fourteen language stocks. I also believe they could be traced back even further into four or five language bases. If we could trace them back, I believe we would find that the people of those four bases were on the same boat that arrived here from some other part of the world after the last cleansing. Or possibly they came from two to four different boats.

"After they landed, there were few people and a lot of room, as the different tribes prospered. However, the land had only enough food to sustain so many people in the hunter/gatherer lifestyle. Eventually, the bands became too crowded, causing them to split. But they stayed in contact with one another to the best of their ability. Over time, the language grew into distinct dialects. Some groups had become so far apart that they didn't see each other for thousands and thousands of years. If they did meet up again, they may have found only a few words, out of the whole language, that were even remotely similar. Possibly the language evolved so much that blood relatives met each other after eons and couldn't understand anything the other said. In any case, it is a natural way for things to progress."

(In support of Gram's point, consider the difference in slang between the North and the South in our country. During the Vietnam War, when I first went into the army fresh from Wisconsin I was sent to South Carolina, where I had a tough time talking with the people from the deep southern states. I could hardly understand anything the sergeants were saying except "ge' down" and "gi'me ten.")

The Heart Box

When we were taking a break from gathering herbs to eat a sandwich, my gram would tell me stories and legends. This is one of them:

When the Creator made man and woman, he made us perfect. As he looked us over, he made a little void in between our lungs, our backbone, and our heart. He thought about what he should do with this void.

"I know," he thought, "I will create a little 'heart box' in that void for everyone. The heart box will be the source of a person's love for other people and for me, the Creator, and it will also be the place for people to store their traumas and heavy emotions for a few days, until they are ready to give them to me."

However, the Creator created the heart box *before* he blew life into us. After we were alive, guess what we did first as a speaking species? We started whining: "We need light so we can see, and dark so we can sleep; we need to know what is food and what do we do when we are thirsty, and how do we stay warm when it's cold, and what is medicine and what poison, and where do we find shelter and for crumb sake where is the Home Depot??"

The Creator said, "Listen, all of you. This is very important, so pay attention: you are my children and I love you, and so I give you free will. You have the power to choose between positive and negative; remember to let no one take that away from you, as I will not. But I advise you to concentrate on the positive and give the negative to me."

As the Creator soon found, though, once we put stuff into our heart box it almost takes dynamite to get it out. It's our junk and we are going to hang on to it at all cost, no matter what it does to us.

We humans tend to hang on to too much baggage such as anger, guilt, and pain. We tend to keep inside the hurts and sorrows from losses of family and friends. We also hang onto other life losses such as money and material things. That little place the Creator gave us to store our hurts was meant to be used for just a short while, until we were ready to let them go. But instead, we stuff our heart boxes with more and more hurts and traumas until we learn from our life's lessons or die. We may often carry this baggage for many lifetimes if we don't learn to let it go.

The heart box is like any other box. If it becomes too full, it breaks. Let's say you and your spouse each come home with a one-pound sack of potatoes. You put your potatoes into a one-pound box and it becomes full. Then your spouse wants to put his bag of potatoes in the box, as well. So he, being a guy, forces the potatoes into the box, causing the sides to crack. You don't want the box to break, so your spouse runs to the garage and returns with some boards, nails, and a hammer. He then proceeds to reinforce the sides of the box. And hey, guess what happens! You really *can* put two pounds of potatoes in a one-pound box. The problem is that the potatoes get mashed up in the process.

Now, trying to keep too many potatoes in too small a space is just like what happens when we store more and more things in the heart box. Eventually, everything gets mashed. That's what we do to ourselves in the process.

It just so happens that the closest organ to the heart box is the heart. The heart pumps blood to our lungs and throughout our bodies. If the heart box swells too much, the pump can't work and the lungs can't move. This causes us to have difficulty breathing.

25

Have you ever noticed that, when you experience a sudden trauma, such as witnessing an accident or a relationship breakup, the first thing that happens is that you have trouble breathing and your heart physically hurts? And that then, after a short while, you can catch your breath and the pain in your heart goes away?

What has happened is that, at first, the addition of the new trauma has caused the heart box to swell, so that it presses uncomfortably against the heart and lungs. But then, in an unconscious ability the Creator gave us, we have stolen energy from our own cells to build a wall around our heart box, just as the man reinforced the potato box so that it could hold more potatoes. Reinforced by the stolen energy, the swelling of the heart box is reduced, and the heart box returns to a size small enough for the heart to pump without hurting and the lungs to breathe easily again. Essentially, this process allows us to compact more and more negative things, whatever they may be, into our heart boxes (the world's first trash compactors).

For the most part, we men start with our shoulders and then move to our lower backs to steal energy to contain the things we put in our heart boxes, or it can happen in reverse order. Women seem to steal their energy from the Mother's Cross, those lines drawn from the base of the skull to just above the bra line and from the center of the shoulder blade to the center of the other shoulder blade.

The problem is that, when we draw on our cellular energy to reinforce our heart boxes, we weaken our cells. Weakening our cells weakens our aura as a whole and makes it easier for disease, weakened bones, weakened immune systems, and weakened emotional states to take hold in our bodies. I think everyone knows about the heart box, but most people don't realize that the tightness they feel within their chest is from it.

One good way to unload our heart boxes is through the Oneida Fire Ceremony. The ceremony's main function is for us to give all our painful memories and traumas to the Creator. We do this through writing things down and offering them up in prayer. This ritual helps us to heal and get stronger.

In the process, we uncover ever and ever deeper old hurts. You can think of the heart box and its memories being like a pile of CDs (or, if you want to date yourself, 45-rpm records) all stacked up. As we give our painful memories to the Creator, we are, in essence, removing these recordings. This, in turn, uncovers other and older records of memories that slowly creep upward into our subconscious minds and then filter into consciousness. Often after a fire ceremony our emotions are quite intense, and it is the uncovering these old records that causes the intensity. After all, such records are of painful memories that we have intentionally covered over, sometimes for many years, in order not to deal with them. When they finally come up, the feelings can last a week or more. If you don't believe it, just try it. And as those old thoughts and memories emerge, write them down and make them the basis of your next ceremony.

If you write things down in the fire ceremony, complete the ritual, and they *still* come back again, don't worry. It just means that you have stored those memories in your heart box more than one time.

Once a sixty-three-year-old woman came to me for healing. She didn't know me, so on the first healing I explained the fire ceremony to her and mentioned that she had old stuff she needed to let go of because it did no good for her to hang on to it. I never mentioned what the old stuff was because I didn't want to scare her on the first visit. By her third healing, she had done sixteen fire ceremonies. The day of her third healing, afterward she dutifully went home and did her seventeenth. About 9:30 p.m. she called, crying, and said, "This one thing always comes back no matter how many times I burn the damn thing."

I could hear the tears falling as we talked. I said to her, "This is about your being raped when you were fifteen, isn't it?"

For a second there was no crying—no sound at all, in fact, from the phone—just stunned silence. "How on earth did you know that?" she asked.

"I've known since day one, but I felt you didn't trust me enough at the time to confide in me. But I think you trust me now, so I brought it up."

"Why won't it go away?"

"Well," I answered, using my above analogy, "our heart boxes are a lot like the old juke boxes with the 45 rpm records all stacked up neat; the little arm would come down, pick up a record, play it, and then pick up the next one and play it, and so on. Let's say you are the lady filling the juke box and you just love Elvis."

"How did you know that . . . ahh . . . never mind."

I continued. "So you take Elvis records and put one in every other record slot. What happens? You keep hearing Elvis over and over again. Now equate this process to the heart box. You do a fire ceremony and burn up the big E, and what shows up for the next fire ceremony? Of course, the big E plays over and over until you get to the bottom record."

"But why would I put him in there so much?" the woman asked.

"Okay, here we go for a short lesson in history. You were raped when you were fifteen, and it took some time to get over. But by sixteen you had healed a bit, and you met this really nice boy. He asked you out, and what is the first thing you do? You take out that rape—that record—you had buried, and you look at it. Then you place it on top of the pile of records, so that now, not only is it on *top* of the pile, it is also still down at the *bottom* from where you pulled it out. But you don't want it to be on top, so you go out and find some minor traumas to put over it so that you can't see it again.

You may even have to make minor arguments with friends or family, because they are easier to take than the real pain you are burying.

"Things are flowing fairly smoothly for you, and then you break up with your boyfriend. What do you do now? Why, you pull the rape out yet again and place it on top to see if you were damaged goods and if the rape was the reason why the break-up happened. But of course it wasn't, so again you bury it.

"Then, later, you are out of school and meet the man you are going to marry. The first thing you do is look at the rape again to see if you are worthy. The answer is, of course you are. You did nothing wrong as a kid; you had no control over a vile, wounded pedophile. But by now, you have stacked that rape up in your heart box maybe twenty times from looking at it at different stages of your life. However, to get rid of it, you need only to keep on doing the fire ceremony. Keep sending the rape to the Creator and, I promise, when you get down to the bottom record of it, it will be gone. So keep on keeping on."

I received a phone call from the woman about a week later.

"It took twenty-three fire ceremonies, but it is really gone! Thank you, thank you, thank you. I can't say it enough."

She was a very happy girl when she got past her memory of that rape, I must say. It has been ten years since this lady had to do that many fire ceremonies. But she is still doing them for other things, and she told me she wished she would have learned of this ceremony when she was thirty.

My personal belief is that each person is a healer of sorts. It is much like baseball. Everyone in the world can pick up a ball and throw it, even though not everyone is Babe Ruth. Likewise, everyone can participate in their own healing. If people would give their attention to the fire ceremony and let go of the things that bother them, it would be much easier for them to be healthier and happier.

For example, when a loved one passes away, hold onto the love and the good memories. But be sure to give all your pain of the crossing to the Creator, or God, or whatever you call your higher power. When you hold the pain in your heart box, it weakens your body, your entire immune system, and your aura.

I am sure that almost every person in the world knows by now what an aura is. But some people don't know that our auras are made of the projections of the energy around each and every cell in our bodies, not unlike the light that fiber-optic lamps project. As I said, the Creator gave us the ability to draw energy from our own cells to reinforce the heart-box walls. When that energy is lost, you lose the protection of the energy field or aura around you, and you get sick.

This is not to say that the Creator's intention was for us to overload our heart boxes in the manner that we all often do. But at the same time, we shouldn't feel guilty about having done so. Again, when the Creator made us, he made us perfect as we are. If we remember that we are perfect as we are, then we are not so inclined to judge against ourselves.

The Oneida Fire Ceremony

As I have explained, I discovered that the most important aid to healing ourselves is the Oneida Fire Ceremony, which involves writing down your prayers and burning the paper so that your prayers ascend to the Creator. My grandmother passed down to me the following version of the fire ceremony:

"In the days of my grandmother's grandmother," said Gram, "there was no paper to write on, so the people had to gather the materials they needed for a ceremony from the woods. First they gathered pieces of birch bark and thinned them down to two or three layers to make the bark pliable enough to fold. Then they found mineral stones to grind into powder and mix with elk or buffalo fat for paint. With this mixture, they painted symbols, pictographs, or petroglyphs on the birch bark to represent what they wanted or what they needed to let go of. In the swamps where the black spruce grew, they would harvest its small, fine, red roots and weave them into red cloth to wrap the ceremonial birch bark in. They gathered nettles and soft maple bark. They boiled the bark to make a purple dye for the cordage made from the nettle. The cordage was used to tie off the red cloth. Of course, they used tobacco, the medicine that is essential to every native ceremony. It was placed inside the painted birch-bark paper after a prayer was made. The paper was then folded up and wrapped in the red cloth and tied up with the purple cord before burning.

"So, you can see that it took a lot of work to prepare for the fire ceremony in the old days. Now that we have pen and paper, it is easy to take this important ceremony for granted. Today, we only have to be department-store hunters and gatherers. When it took weeks or more to prepare for a fire ceremony, people held it in much higher esteem, as we still should."

Grandma asked, "Do you remember how I showed you to breathe?"

"Yes," I replied.

"Well, remember to tell your clients to breathe into the Earth Mother, like I showed you."

Here is what Gram taught me: Essentially, you are bringing the energy up your arms. As you inhale, raise your arms and draw the energy from your fingertips to let it flow into your central core. At the same time, use your mind to push the energy down through your core, out the bottom of your feet, and into the earth.

Then, as you exhale, the Earth Mother removes the negative energy, or whatever you want to let go of, and sends good energy back to fill you up, which instantly relieves any tension. She sends positive energy to replace the negative because she always works to achieve a balance. This simple exercise *will* help you stay in balance; and if you are in balance, you will find that everything in life becomes easier.

Breathing into the earth can be done in any position: standing, sitting, or lying down. As you use your breath, imagine it as a valve. As you breathe into your lungs, the air pushes the negative out and down. As you breathe out, the air and energy come up and out your lungs, drawing new energy from the Earth Mother. It may be helpful to imagine the breath as a yellow line of energy, much like the graphic lines used to point out movement in a football instant replay on TV. I find that image works well for many people.

"You can't take the air out of a balloon without the balloon getting smaller," said Gram. "The Creator set it up so that when the Earth Mother takes the negative, she always replaces it with positive so that we don't die."

"Grandma," I said, "what if I can't do this healing stuff, or I don't want to, when I get big?"

"Don't worry," she said. "You can and you will. Just remember all the things I teach you and know that the Creator is the one who does the healing by sending you his energy. All you do is pass it on."

My Version of the Fire Ceremony

This ceremony is a forgiveness ceremony. It is about forgiving yourself, others, situations, and other things that have hurt you in your life. Gram freely gave the ceremony to me, and it is in this faith that I give it to you. No one should charge to help people do this ceremony. You will lose the spirit of the ceremony if you charge, and let no one charge you. With that said, here goes:

1. The first thing you have to do is ask God—or the Creator, or whatever you happen to call your Higher Power—to help you forgive yourself. You do this by writing requests to him on paper.

    This process includes asking God to help you forgive yourself for situations in which you had no control, such as your place of birth, what your life was like as you grew up, parental break-ups or deaths in the family, and so on. We need to do this, because, on a deep, subconscious level, we hold ourselves accountable for these things. We are a great species for blaming ourselves. Say our grandpa passes away. We say things like, "Jeez, if I had only stopped by last night, maybe he would still be here." Or, "If I had called, then I would have known something was wrong." I am here to tell you that, as it says in the Bible, no man knows the day, hour, or minute of his passing. But when the Creator wants us home, it's our time. When the second hand gets back to twelve, it's over, and there is nothing in the universe that can stop it. Therefore, there is no reason to blame yourself; death just *is*, plain and simple.

So now, think back on your own life. What has hurt you today over which you had absolutely no control? Then think about yesterday, last week, last year, and so on, and list as many things as you can think of that you could not possibly have changed. Don't worry if you miss something; this is not a one-shot ceremony. I recently did my sixty-first fire ceremony with a group of vets from the Minneapolis Veterans Administration. Most think they got more out of the ceremony than they had in a week of therapy.

2. Next, ask God to help you forgive yourself for situations in which you *did* have some control and did not act according to your highest light. We say things we don't mean; and, though they may feel good at the time, guess whose heart box they end up in?

   However, even when we do not act according to our highest light, it is because we are in fact human—with our human emotions, reason, and frailties—and that is okay, because the Creator made us this way and loves us. And again, because of the way we are wired, we tend to hold these things against ourselves. But carrying a load that doesn't belong to us does not lead to healing; so we need to let go of the things over which we *did* have control as well as the things over which we didn't, when holding on no longer helps us with our highest good. Situations in which we have control could be our own relationship break-ups, arguments with loved ones, and letting alcohol cloud our judgment.

   I find that, usually, we hold onto the junk for dear life rather than give it up. I'm not sure if this is because we don't know how easy it is to get rid of old hurts, pains, and traumas, or if it is just inherent human greed. Most of us fight against greed, but some embrace it—even when what they're clinging to is harmful to them.

3. Now ask God to help you forgive places, situations, and other people that have hurt you. The more we hold onto our hurt over these things, the more energy we use that we could be using for our healing. Again, think back to today, yesterday, the day before that, and so on. Think of as many negative things as you can to release, because the more you can let go of, the more you strengthen your energy field, which is your protection.

   Don't be afraid to thank the Creator in advance for answering your prayer, and be specific in your wording of what you want (for example, freedom from resentment, health, spiritual healing, and so on). If it is good for you, the Creator will usually provide.

4. As you talk to the Creator, thanking him for helping you in this process of forgiveness, hold your tobacco up and put your prayers into it. Then put the tobacco holding your prayers into the middle of the paper on which you have written your needs, and crumple the paper around the tobacco. That way, your words enclose the tobacco, and, when you burn it, the smoke carries them right to the Creator.

5. Wrap this bundle of paper and tobacco in a red cotton cloth that is six-to-seven-inches square (or whatever size feels right). This is so God the Creator knows you are serious and is the way my grandmother taught me. Tie the cloth with a purple strip of cloth, string, or yarn. Tie it with four knots.

Purple is the color of healing. The four knots represent the Four Grandfathers, who are the Creator's spirit helpers. They watch the north, east, south, and west.

6. Throw the healing bundle into a hot, friendly fire so that you can see the smoke taking the words to the Creator. A hot, friendly fire is one where the wood has burned down to coals. I use the fire pit outside my house. On days when I don't have time to build a fire, I use a two-pound coffee can. I poke holes in the side of the can near the bottom with a can opener that my dad used to open beer with (or a "church key," for those of you old enough to remember). I then place four or five pieces of Match Light charcoal in the can and light them. Next I fill out my writing for the ceremony, and by the time I'm finished and have my bundle made, the charcoal is white hot; all I have to do is drop the bundle in. I sometimes don't have the patience I should have, and I think this way of doing the ceremony would be helpful to those of you who are like me. (I have as much patience as a drip of water, and you know how much that is: once the drip starts, nothing on earth can stop it.)

Don't be surprised if, a short while after the fire ceremony, you notice yourself feeling weepy, angry, sad, elated, happy, or any number of other emotions. As you peel the layers off old memories that you had hidden from yourself deep in the unconscious, the old wounds start to float up into consciousness again, and you begin feeling the emotions that you have covered for such a long time. So keep a little notebook to write about things as they come up. It will be the basis for your next fire ceremony. Soon you will have plenty of material for the next one. I have noticed that this pattern has recurred with my clients over and over, time and again, during the last forty-five years. (If you are a healer, it's great if you can conduct the ceremony with a bunch of people around a bonfire all at once, but with my client load, I just don't have the time.)

The fire ceremony is not a thing to fear; instead, it is a way to overcome fear. It is also a way to enrich your present life by ridding it of past-life issues—issues that we carry from life to life until we deal with them, as they won't go away on their own. The fire ceremony cleans out your heart box, giving you a much greater opportunity to achieve a healthy mind, soul, and body.

I heard of a man who did our ceremony and is now charging people to do it for them. That's a nice thought, but the only one who can truly cleanse the heart box is oneself. I can help people pull negative stuff out, but it will never *stay* out unless they do the fire ceremony for themselves. Otherwise, the issue they're trying to get rid of will be back in a matter of hours, or four days at most, and that is only if the facilitator knows about wrapping the client in a cocoon of light after a healing is over (more about this later).

We can't be lazy people; we have to do the work ourselves if we want to heal. Don't waste money on someone claiming they can do something they can't. There is no magic pill that fixes anything without work on our part. The Creator gave us the tools to work with—let's use them. The fire ceremony is not hard to do. If you can't do it by the end of the book, come see me and I will show you!

As I have said, my gram taught me that Oneida breathing is an important tool to use with the fire ceremony to balance the emotions, help ground us, and convert negative energy to positive. It is to be done four times a day with four repetitions each time, if you so choose. Here is a quick recap of how to do it:

Stand with both feet on the floor and inhale deeply through your nose. Visualize your negative energy going down your body, out your feet, and into the ground. Then exhale through your mouth and visualize positive energy coming up from the earth, through your feet, and into the rest of your being. Upon inhaling, you send your negative energy to the Earth Mother; upon your exhale, she replaces the negative with new, positive energy.

The Colors of Healing

My grandmother and I were sharing breakfast as my young brain brought a question to mind. "Gram, isn't the healing light the same for everyone?"

"The light the Creator sends you may or may not be in the same colors as those of other healers," she answered. "The light the Creator sends me is somewhat different from my mother's. Hers was first yellow, then purple, then green. Your colors may be the same or different from ours. Every light has its own vibration. The vibration, or frequency, works entirely differently for each person."

"What's *frequency*?" I asked.

"Frequency is the speed that things move or vibrate at."

"How will I know?"

"How will you know what?" she asked.

"What my colors are."

"It may take a while for you to see the colors, so what you need to do is this: First, start with a prayer in mind, asking the Creator to send the healing light that stimulates the cells to release negative things or energy in the body.

"Second, ask the Creator to send the healing light that does the repair work, making sure not to miss any part of the body.

"Third, after you do that for a while, ask the Creator to send you the light to wrap the body, as a caterpillar wraps itself in threads. Just as the caterpillar's threads have to dry to keep it safe, the cocoon we wrap critters and people in has to set up to keep the healing in. Keep in mind that each color has a different vibrational frequency, and each frequency will resonate with each person differently on each particular problem you work on. Therefore, your colors will more than likely be specific to you as an individual."

So my grandmother taught me in my youth. As an adult, I now know that each of us perceives differently. My perceptions were guided by Gram, but by no means are they the same for everyone. And, if people do their grounding to Mother Earth through their breathing and the Oneida Fire Ceremony, they will extend their healing for weeks.

The Legend of the Seven Sisters (the Pleiades)

I was moping about how long things take and how slowly time moves. To comfort me, Gram said, "Time will pass quicker than you can think. I felt the same way you do when I was a girl, and now look—I'm sixty-six years old already!"

"No, Gram! You are sixty-six years young! I don't know of anybody who could keep up with you!" I enthused.

"Thank you, but I'm not sure that's completely true," she said, smiling.

"Didn't it seem like forever to you when your gram told you how long it would be before you could start healing?"

"Surely it did, but the years went by so fast that when the time did come, I thought I wasn't ready, just like you will in the future.

"Concerning the future," Gram went on, "many years from now you will hear people talking about being spokespeople for the people of the Pleiades, the Seven Sisters. You will hear that the people from the Pleiades are different from humans. But originally, we came from the Pleiades; that was our first home." She then told me this legend:

In the days so far back that no one can remember them, we the Oneidas lived on a different Turtle Island from this one, on another planet in another star system: the Seven Sisters system, or the "Pleiades," as it is also called. *Turtle Island* is the Oneida name for the continent. The Turtle Island on the other planet was like North America on Earth, but because we forgot to take care of her, she became trashed to the point where she rebelled against us. It rained nonstop for weeks and weeks. The ground was so wet that it could hold no more water. Everything was flooding, and the people fled to a huge, pointed mountaintop. It was much bigger than anything we have on the Turtle Island on this planet. All the people from the tribe ran up the mountain as the water kept rising. Finally, only the peak of the mountain was left above the water. It was a few hundred yards tall with hundreds of people on it. Soon the mountain started rumbling and shaking, and the people were screaming in terror. Then, with a big *whoosh*, the mountain blew her top and went skyward, with the people still on it as flames and molten rock trailed behind.

It traveled for a very long time, until it landed ever so gently on yet another planet in the sky. The people looked around at their new home and liked it. Eons before they landed there, the Creator had seeded it with everything they would need to survive. The people called their new home the Sky Nation. They lived there for many, many generations before, in turn, one woman fell to our own Earth to start populating our own Turtle Island. It was not until then that Earth became our home.

"Remember this legend always, so that you, too, can tell your grandchildren," Gram concluded. "And remember, originally our people came from the Pleiades. If people want to know what people from the Pleiades think, they should see us, since we are the Pleiadians' descendants. You will hear many people say they speak for us, but it will be all hogwash. They will make up all kinds of things about our ancestors that are not true. It will be rabble talking. Remember, in all cases they will just be trying to make some money. Of course, such people have to live, and it will probably cost more to live by that time, but remember: they will just be telling false stories to make a sale to the unknowing."

This caution reminds me to emphasize that the stories my grandmother told me were not from children's books; they were the oral legends of our people. They have been preserved through storytelling and passed from generation to generation for eons. The next legend is the full story about how we, the Oneida, came to live on this earth.

The Legend of Sky Woman

"Long ago," Gram began, "there was nothing here on earth except darkness and a world full of water. But there *was* a Sky Nation way, way high up in the sky. The people had light up there, and trees and grass and all manner of creatures that the Creator had made for them. They had food and clothing, and a sky chief always led the people in peace and love.

"This sky chief had a daughter who was vain and had to prove her beauty all the time. She had no need to, because anyone who saw her could see how beautiful she was. It came to pass that the sky chief's daughter was with child—twins, in fact. One day she decided to prove to herself how beautiful she was, even in pregnant state, by coercing a few braves into trying to pull of the ground an enormous tree out that grew not far from the edge of the sky world. First one guy tried, then another and another and another; but still, no one could make the huge tree come up or even fall.

"Seeing the commotion, the sky chief asked what was going on, and the braves told him they were doing it for his daughter. The sky chief was so angry that he grabbed the tree himself and, with a mighty tug, ripped it out of the ground. When the people looked down into the hole the tree left, they saw the dark blue globe of the earth miles and miles below. The chief ordered that no one was to go near the hole for fear of dropping to their death. Everyone listened and stayed away except for one. Do you know who?"

"The chief's daughter." I said.

"That's right. The chief's daughter sneaked out and crept up to the hole very slowly so no one would see her. She kneeled on her leather dress and stared down into the darkness for the longest time, until her eyes adjusted. And then she saw it: the dark blue globe. She was content to sit on her knees and watch it for hours. After a very long time, she heard someone coming. Fearing it might be her father, she got up too quickly and her legs wouldn't work. They were asleep and wouldn't move. Then the bank of the hole started slowly caving off, moving ever more near her. She got one leg to move back a little, and more of the bank caved off and fell into the nothingness below. Her other leg moved very quickly, and it looked like she was going to be safe, when suddenly a great big piece of the bank dropped and tumbled away.

"'EEEEOOOOOOOOOOOOOOOoouuuuuuuu,' the chief's daughter cried, with her voice trailing off and her hair standing on end.

"She screamed for the longest time as she went down and down and down. When she finally stopped screaming, she could see the dark blue planet far, far below, getting ever closer. Fumbling for her tobacco, she started praying to the great, all-powerful Creator. 'If you can find it in your heart to forgive me,' she prayed, 'I will forget my vain ways and be a good mother to these twins I am going to have.' She soon found that, if she grabbed her sleeves and spread her legs, her dress slowed her descent. And the little blue globe was getting ever bigger.

"As she got closer, she was sure she was done for, because she realized that she was looking at water just like in the Sky Nation; but, unlike there, on this globe there was no end to it. She started praying again, making all the prayers she thought might help, as she fell and fell. She was dropping so fast that she had a hard time hanging on to her tobacco. When she had fallen to three times the height of our tallest tree, she thought that was the last sight she would ever see . . . "

In one of those weighty Native American pauses, Gram became silent, making me anxious.

"Just then, though, four great swans grabbed the woman's dress corners and sleeves and stopped her fall."

To my clapping, Gram scolded, "Calm down so you can hear!" Then she went on, "The swans flew around with the woman for the longest time. After hours of flying, they finally came to a great turtle that floated in the ocean and was so large you could not see its other side or length. The swans eventually set her down on the edge of the turtle's back, not far from the water. This great turtle was as big as a continent, swimming in an endless body of water. This was before Turtle Island and South Turtle Island were hooked together by the land that would become Central America.

"The chief's daughter—whom we know as Sky Woman—was cold without sunlight and lonesome in the dark. But fortunately she had her bag with her, and in her bag was some tobacco. She stood with her tobacco and thanked the Creator for saving her and asked if she could have some sunlight. After she finished her prayer, she put her tobacco down. The sky started to turn pink in the east. (It was not the same east as ours, though, as the world turned the other way in those days. Everything was reversed, and what is now west was then east.)

"Soon there was full light in the sky, and Sky Woman said to the Creator, 'O Creator of all things, I need help. I can't live on this barren shell. I won't be able to grow food or have shelter or make new clothing.' Soon she was surrounded by animals, who all talked to her. In those days, the animal people and real people could still communicate with each other because they spoke the same language.

When she asked the animals for help, they all offered. First, the mighty builder, the beaver, said that he would go to the bottom and bring up some earth for the woman to grow food in. He then dived into the water. He was gone all of the first day, all of the second day, and all of the third day. On the fourth day, his body came up without any earth. Then the woman asked, 'Is there anyone else who could try?' The otter volunteered but failed. The loon was next to volunteer, saying, 'I am the best diver here; if I can't do it, no one can.' While the woman and the other animals waited and waited, the great diver dove down, down into the deep. He, too, was gone the first day and the second, only to reappear on the third morning. Gasping for breath, the loon said, 'I couldn't do it. I tried, and it can't be done! The water is too deep for anyone to touch the bottom.'

"'Isn't there *anyone* here who can help me?' cried Sky Woman.

"A wee, small voice in the back of the crowd said, 'I will.' When they all looked around, they saw that the only one standing there was the little muskrat. 'I will help you,' he repeated. All the other animals jeered, saying, 'If the mighty builder couldn't help, and the mighty diver couldn't, what, little one, makes you think that you can?'

"The muskrat simply smiled and said, 'I will try.'

"And down he went, only to reappear the next morning. When asked if he had brought some earth he said no—he just had to catch his breath. More jeering. But after the muskrat had caught his breath, down he went again.

"He, too, was gone for a total of three days. But on the morning of the fourth day, his little body floated up. In his little, dead hand was a small bit of earth, which Sky Woman put on the back of the great turtle.

"Soon the small bit of earth spread, growing on its own—from where the sun rises to where it sets, from where it is always warm to where it is always cold. And as the earth spread, trees came up, and grass, and soon herds of buffalo, deer, and elk followed, and the land was covered with all manner of animals and birds, and the birds sang joyous songs. The woman said to the Creator, 'I need water so I can drink and food so I can eat. I need dark so I can sleep and light so I can work. I need to know what foods are safe, what plants are poison and what are medicine, how to make shelter for when my babies come. . . .'

"'I will give you everything you need,' interrupted the Creator, 'but there will be a price: You must take care of the things I make for you. You are to respect them, cherish them, and remember who your Creator is. First, I will give you four medicines.

"'The first medicine is sage. You may burn the sage to smudge yourself so that you are pure when you pray to me; otherwise, I will not hear you as well as I could.

"'The second medicine is tobacco. I give this so that you can hold it up to me in offering when you pray. That way, I will know you are coming to me with a good mind and a good heart. If you do not hold your tobacco up to me, I will not know if you have a good mind; you may not be right in the head. So I will never be sure if I can answer you, as you might not know what you are asking for.

"'The third medicine is sweetgrass. I give this to you to smudge with and to draw good spirits to you as helpers. Pay attention to these spirits, as they will bring gifts and answers from me. When you need an answer, burn the sweet grass and make four circles with it as you think of your question; then my helpers will know that you are the one in need of an answer, and they will come.

"'The fourth medicine is flat-needle cedar, or white cedar. This I give you to make smudge with when you have coughs. Make tea out of it when you feel ill. And you *will* feel ill, as I know you will put too much stuff in your heart box.'"

Gram said, "This is why we use the medicines we use—in honor of the teachings of our first ancestor, Sky Woman, and what she taught the children." Then she went on:

"'Do these things,' said the Creator, 'and you will have a good life. Forget to honor the Earth Mother as I have taught you, and all manner of ills will befall you. I love you. You and your descendants are my children and I will be patient with you; but if you harm any of my creations, I will not stop them from fighting back to protect themselves. I gave them free will also, as they, too, are my children. Pay attention to these teachings, and pass them on to all your generations.'"

People Discover What We Have Always Known

One bright summer morning, Gram and I were sitting at her little blonde oak table before we went to gather herbs. Gram was teaching once again, and I was listening.

"Remember the Creator's telling Sky Woman about the importance of honoring the Earth Mother and all her creatures—a lesson that modern society has largely lost. But in the future, as the world population grows the time will near when people will reawaken about the need to take care of Mother Earth. Then you will notice that the signs I told you about will come at a faster pace all the time. Don't worry; the Creator always provides enough time to do everything we need to do. When you get to be toward my age, you will notice that the days get much longer, but the years fly by like leaves in the wind. The number of your clients will greatly increase. You will also find more people to apprentice under you. You will see a shift in people's attitudes. People will be more open and receptive while discovering a "new" thing: *energy work*. This is something we have known about forever, but they will try, like they always have, to pick it apart and to make it their own, just like they did about discovering America. And, for the most part, they will think that they are doing the healing and forget that no healing happens except through the Creator. So, my son, keep love in your heart for your Creator; do his bidding, and he will do yours. Watch and remember the things I have said."

"I will; I promise, Gram."

As I sit here writing and thinking, I find the things I learned from Gram amazing. She was so wise for someone with only a third-grade education. But then again, her education came from nature. I spent a lot of time with her in the woods, but that was nothing compared to the amount of time she had spent with her own grandmother. Even though I didn't grow up in the kind of community setting Gram had experienced as a child, she herself sure did the best she could with me. It would have been great to have had more time with her, but, in Gram's words, "It is what it is."

Another thing I will always credit her for is that she gave me the means to find my own answers for problems that medical science didn't even understand at the time.

Once, for instance, I worked with an old woman who came to me with arthritis. During our conversation, she mentioned that she used to have a heart murmur—the "half-beat," so to speak. I checked the woman and found scar tissue on the side of the node in the right atrium of the heart that creates electrical currents to make our hearts beat regularly. It seems that, until the woman was sixty-five, her heart skipped a beat every once in a while. Suddenly, when she turned sixty-five, the murmur disappeared.

Later that day a male client came in with the same problem, and we discussed the heart murmur of the old woman I had seen earlier. While I was checking the man's node, it misfired. Because of the way Gram had taught me to think for myself and rely on the Creator, and based on the electrical work I had done as a contractor, I understood that this misfiring caused what I call a "short cycle." A short cycle means that the node producing the electrical current that drives the blood through the heart does not complete its circuit as it should do, resulting in a very rapid heartbeat. This understanding helped me heal the man. Eventually medical science proved my hypothesis about the short cycle right. If it weren't for my grandma, I wouldn't have known what questions to ask the client or the Creator.

"Now, listen to me, Russell," Gram said. "When you start to do healings in a couple of years on little birdies, dogs, and cats, you have to ask the Creator what the matter is. You also have to do several things to make the healing work.

"First, you have to know that the Creator is going to do the healing. Second, you have to thank the Creator for doing the healing, and you have to do whatever the Creator says. Always keep an intention of healing, and if you *know* the Creator can do it instead of just *believing* he can do it, then you are halfway there; the other half comes from our human clients as they practice Oneida breathing and do the fire ceremony." (The fire ceremony is thousands and thousands of years old. As far as Gram knew, the people had always done it. I was six or seven when she told me this.)

Gram was really good at reiterating things. I thought it was because she was old, but I realize now that it was because she didn't want me to forget. She wanted to drive the teachings into my head, to make sure that I passed them on correctly. So, for instance, she would say again, "This ceremony was passed on to me by my grandmother, who got it from her grandmother, who got it from hers, and so on. I'm sure you are getting the picture."

In turn, I give this teaching to my apprentices and clients. In fact, I used to teach a course on the Oneida Fire Ceremony at the University of Wisconsin in Menomonie, usually every two to three years. I did this during the Body, Mind, and Spirit Conference, which is held annually at the end of October. The weekend was always extremely fun and I often ran into some very talented, gifted young people. Their first question was usually, "Can I really do this?"

I always told them, as I tell all who ask, that anyone can heal. It is just like playing baseball: almost everyone can swing a bat and hit the ball. To be sure, though, not everyone is Babe Ruth, and the Babe Ruths are the ones I usually look for in apprentices. I want people who will become more proficient than I am.

Is the polar shift that began in 2012, as my gram explained, going to play out, as some people say? If so, in the near future, many healers will be needed. I figure that about one or two will be needed for every village.

The people who live tribally now will be better off than those who have had technology and lost it. The old saying "you can't lose something you never had" will prove true to the benefit of country folks—those who know how to grow food and make things and can get by with less rather than more. We never know what the future holds. I know no more than anyone else. All I can say for sure is that we are not taking care of Mother Earth, and she has the same free will as the Creator gave us. Will she cleanse herself? I hope we start taking care of her so that we don't have to find out.

So I urge you, for your own enlightenment and the welfare of yourself and others, to open your mind and heart. Learn about the fire ceremony, and together we can heal.

Visions Explained My Way

I am a person who believes in visions and the old way. Dreams, visions, and sightings have come to me intermittently since I was three-and-a-half. Years may go by with none, and then I might have several in a month. Visions occur when they are needed. The message or information may be personal, directed to me, or it may be meant for broadcasting to the greater world.

I was about forty years old when I had a vision of myself walking through an old-growth forest of huge trees. I heard a baby crying and walked toward the sound. As I walked through dappled sunlight coming down in little columns, I spotted what appeared to be a young girl. She had a cradle board in her hands, and I noticed that the crying was coming from within it. The girl's arm looked like that of a fifteen-year-old. As I walked up to her around the huge tree, she was turned away. All I could see was the back of her head.

When I asked if I could see the baby, the girl turned to look at me. I was startled, as she had the look of someone who was a million years old. She said in a young voice, "Of course you can see her; she needs you. She is crying because she is in pain." The mother pulled the blanket back from the top of the cradle board, and I saw the baby's head turned away from me. When it finally turned toward me I was startled again, as the baby was older than the mother. Then the baby looked at me and spoke of an ancient wisdom.

"You have to tell the people that they must take care of me, or heed this warning: I will rid myself of you all like a dog shaking fleas off its back. I have rid myself of people three times before, and it is not a hard thing to do, because you humans are so frail. I don't want to rid myself of you, but I will do whatever I have to do in order to survive."

I responded, "There are many people in high places who could get the message out more easily than I can—actors, politicians, and even presidents." But she said no, that it had to be a common person, preferably a healer, who does the Creator's work.

This vision confused me for a few weeks before I figured out that I had been talking with Mother Earth (the baby) and Mother Nature (the mother). I left the vision feeling uneasy and very much unqualified for the job that Mother Earth had set before me.

Yet it was not hard for me to believe Mother Earth had spoken to me, because, as I have said, in my life visions were common events. In the native tradition they are considered a normal part of life. We indigenous American people have always had visions, as I am sure all other tribal people did before they became mechanized during the Iron Age and Christianity came around. The churches burned people at the stake for having visions, so I am sure that is why accounts of such experiences died out in Europe. I am not laying blame about this; it's not something the white half of me is proud of, but it is what it is.

When, as a three-year-old, I had my very first vision, I woke up from a nightmare, crying. My mother came to my bed and asked what was wrong. I told her that I saw two guys in funny clothes trying to shut Grandpa into a big, gray, metallic suitcase. I had never seen a coffin before, but my dad would travel for work, and when he went on the road he used a steel suitcase. It was the only thing I could liken to what I saw my grandfather lying in. It looked like my dad's suitcase when it was opened, with the divider in it.

And the suitcase holding Grandpa was in a place I had never seen before. I said, "The dirt was black and hard, not like the dirt in our yard [which was red-to-yellowish sand]. The buildings were in rows, and there were so many houses in a row I couldn't believe it. And they didn't have tar paper on the outside. They were made of some hard, square, colorful stones, or they were wood-sided." My Dad would tell me, four days later, that the square little colored stones were clay bricks. One big building I saw had two huge, white trees on either side of the door. I had seen white birch trees before, but these trees were perfectly straight—not bent like birches, at all.

In my vision, my mother carried me as we walked into the building. Many of my relatives were there, and Grandpa George was lying in the big, gray, steel suitcase. Two guys with strips of cloth hanging from their necks (which Dad later told me were ties) wore white shirts and matching black jackets and pants. Having been used to seeing only bib overalls, I was perplexed to see these men wearing suits. They were going to close Grandpa George in that big suitcase. That's when I woke up crying.

My mom said, "Honey, it was just a dream. I talked to Grandpa today and he is fine. He is right across the field, kitty-corner from here."

"Across the field" meant across a forty-acre parcel. Reassured, I went back to sleep.

Just three or four days later, Mom was dressing me in my first pair of new blue jeans and a new shirt. The shirt and jeans were itchy on my skin. Clothes weren't something I was used to; they were too scratchy for me. I was used to being exposed to the sun all the time, as we lived on a dead-end road with only one neighbor. But that day, I was dressed, and my brother and sister also wore new clothes.

I asked my mom, "Where are we going?"

"To town," she answered.

I felt nervous, excited, and scared all at the same time, as this was my first trip to town. I was wearing shoes for the first time ever.

53

(They pinched my toes, and I didn't like having my feet confined that way, at all.)

We all hopped into my dad's black, four-door 1950 Chevy coupe.

When we got to our destination, the building was exactly as I had seen it in my dream. Dad told me those big, white trees were columns that held the porch roof up. My mom picked me up as we all walked into the funeral home. Inside, I saw my aunts and uncles and scads of cousins, just as I had in the vision. The room was packed with people I knew and even people I didn't. And there was Grandma, Grandpa George's widow and my dad's mom. My dad's father, her first husband, had died at the age of seventy-five. That was five years before I was born. Grandpa George was my step-gramps, the only grandpa I had ever known.

As we walked toward the casket, I said, "See, Mom, there are the two guys with their funny clothes and those string things around their necks, and there is Grandpa in that big, gray, steel suitcase."

"So it is," was all my mother said. But later, she related the story of my vision to Gram. I have often wondered if that was the reason Gram chose me as the grandchild to live with her. The vision might have shown her that I was open to learning the healing she would be teaching me.

Once Gram said, "You have to watch everything: not just animals, but your dreams and visions, too. They are all messages in one form or another from the Creator. It is not the Creator's job to give them to us; he just sends them, and it is up to us to catch them. Visions are like words that come at us or that we send. When you speak, you must be careful, because once you send words out, they are no longer yours. They belong to whoever catches them." I send out these words of Gram's here so that now they will belong to you readers. Lessons come at us all the time if we choose not to ignore them.

Everything that happens in a vision feels intensely real. In a spiritual sense, a vision *is* real. It takes place before reality. A vision may arrive close to—or many years before—the real-time event. It can also occur in your sleep or as a kind of waking dream, but it is very different from a typical dream. We all know that a dream we have in our sleep isn't real, while a vision appears to be actually happening in the outside world, and we seem to be living in it. Visions come partly from our subconscious and partly from the Creator or the spirits. Simply put, a vision is a sign of the Creator working with your subconscious mind to solve a problem.

I am sure each of us has had waking dreams in which we see things happen, only some time later to have them come true. If you don't have a word for the experience, know that it is a *vision*, the same as it has always been.

Are visions something to fear? Not on your life. Visions are here to bring messages about things yet to happen or things that happened in the past. They deliver the lessons that may have slipped by us or that we just completely missed. So when a vision appears, know for a fact that it has come at the exact time when you need that particular lesson.

The Child Knows What Others Do Not

In 1955, some two months after my dream of Grandpa's funeral, I woke up crying again. When my mother asked, "What's the matter?" I tried to tell her about the dream I had just been having of a conquistador running a long knife through my back.

She said, "There is no such thing. Now go back to sleep."

"You know, the guys with the pointy steel hats and steel shirts," I persisted.

"Go back to sleep," she repeated. "There's nothing like that." My mom had never heard of conquistadors, having had only a fourth-grade education.

My dream had been a kind of vision of something that took place in about 1519 when Hernan Cortes was invading Mexico. In it, I was the eldest son of Motecahzoma, the king-god of the Aztecs. It was after this dream that I began speaking in the Aztec language, or *Nahuatl* (NA-wah). How I knew it was a mystery, because we had no radio or electricity until 1959—some four years after this dream—and I had had no previous teachings from my parents, my grandmother, or anyone else in the Aztec way of speaking. It just came to me, without my understanding or even caring where the knowledge came from.

The only explanation for such an impressive feat lies in the still-fresh mind of a young child who has not yet been taught by society that he can't access past lives. Something or someone in my dream of the conquistadors had triggered a deep memory, and what had been part of a past life was carried over into the present.

When I began speaking in Aztec, my mother warned me twice before she started washing my mouth out with homemade lye-tallow soap. When I was four—on one of the rare weekends when I was at my folks' place—I was helping mom pull weeds in the garden and explaining what we call *bean* in the Aztec language. My mom said, "You've got to quit speaking that gibberish, or you could get stuck talking that way the rest of your life. Besides, we are Americans and we speak English. Now *stop*, or I'll have to wash your mouth out with the soap I make. I really don't want to, but it will be for your own good."

This was the second time I heard this from her. I figured I was getting to her limit of patience, so I would try to keep from speaking in Aztec, but sometimes it would just slip out. Man, that lye-tallow soap burned like fire! After I tasted it, I soon decided it was better to stop speaking Aztec. Eventually I did stop, but even today I still remember some of the words.

A Young Explorer

In the spring of the year I was to start school, I had not yet turned six. I liked to wander off, so my parents made a deal with me. There was a seven-acre field next to our house, and they said that, as long as I kept the field in sight, I'd be allowed to walk in the woods. I truly loved going out to the woods to watch nature in action. I watched the birds, the squirrels, and especially the deer.

One morning I was walking in the woods by the field. The birds were singing, the sun was bright, and the wind was soft on my face. It was about seven o'clock. As I turned east in the woods, I found myself on a hill overlooking the north end of the field. I saw a doe licking off her second newborn fawn.

As I walked closer, she and the two wobbly-legged fawns ran off the field and down a little valley to the top of the next hill. So, practicing my nature skills, I indianed right up on them. I made it to within fifteen feet or so before spooking them. They were off. They ran down another valley and up to the top of the next hill.

The area called the Casey Mounds was heavily glaciated, leaving lots of hills and valleys. It was considered big for our area—especially big if you are just shy of six years old. The elevation of the hills ranged from four hundred feet to a quarter of a mile high. I followed the fawns to the top of the next hill and was able to get close to them once again. They crossed a narrow valley and went to the top of the next hill, but it was so brushy that I lost them there. After I wandered around and realized that I couldn't find them, I decided to go back to the field.

I walked down and up the three hills and valleys. There was no field! I tried to retrace my steps, but still I found no field. If I had known the size of the chunk of land I was on, which was about five miles wide and seven or eight miles long, I probably would have been concerned. But I didn't know, so I wasn't. Instead, I began exploring and checking out all the wonderful critters that were running around the woods that fine spring day.

As I moved through the woods, I noticed the shadows were getting shorter. Later, I saw they were lengthening. I understood that the shadows indicated that it was getting late. Now I began to worry. In a panic, I began running in no particular direction. I ran until I was nearly exhausted. I began crying. (It is amazing how your mind works when you are not quite six years old.) I then thought, "You have to get ahold of yourself, or you could end up dying out here!"

I decided to walk from tree to tree to make sure I was walking straight. This seemed to work well until I ran into a tall-grass swamp about three hundred yards wide. I looked to the left and to the right; the swamp wound back through the woods as far as I could see in either direction. This made my hair stand up. I wondered, with such a huge swamp around here, why I had never seen it before.

It was then that I heard a drumming sound. It sounded like my dad's old John Deere tractor. In order to start the engine, you turned the big flywheel weight while hearing the pomp-pomp, pomp-pomp until it started—or not; more often not. I decided to go left, in the direction of the drumming sound, in case it was from someone trying to start a tractor.

As I followed the edge of the swamp to the left, I flushed up a ruff grouse, or "partridge," as my dad called them. It seemed I wasn't getting anywhere when, lo and behold, I came to a big, dead white pine. It was surely over one hundred feet tall. I had the idea to use that pine as a marker. With my back to it, I walked to another big tree. I looked back at the dead tree and then walked to another large tree. This system worked for some time, but as I got farther from the swamp, the big white pine kept shrinking, and soon it disappeared. I eventually came to another swamp that extended into the woods in both directions, exactly like the first swamp. This time I headed the other way, to the right.

As the day grew late, I had visions of an old black bear following me. The faster I walked, the more I started to panic. Then I could stand it no more. I ran and ran, until I thought again that I would have to get ahold of myself or I could die.

After following the second swamp for a half hour or so, I came upon another tall, dead white pine. It would have taken six or seven of me, with outstretched arms, to reach around it. I decided to use this tree to navigate through the woods as before, in the hope of finding a road this time. But as I looked at the large tree, I realized it had a broken top—awfully similar to a tree I had seen earlier. When I realized that it must be the *same* tree, the bear scene flashed through my mind. I had visions of a gravestone with my name on it.

This was enough to send me off running. I ran and ran and ran some more, until I was crying and finally collapsed on the forest floor. I was hungry, and my tummy was hurting. In a sobbing, shaky little voice, I asked the Creator to save me. I knew there must be something he needed me to do for him.

"What's the matter?" a voice asked.

"I'm lost," I said without looking up.

"You are not lost," said the voice.

"I am, too," I argued. I looked up to see this old Indian man. He was dressed in buckskin leggings and a leather vest with quill work on it.

"You are not lost, my son," he repeated. "After all, you are *somewhere*, aren't you?" When I heard his words, it all didn't seem so bad, because if you are somewhere, then you are not lost—you are only confused. To be confused instead of being lost seemed so much better. He said, "See those little red berries on the wintergreen? Eat a handful of those, and they will settle your upset belly." I did, and when I was done he said, "Pick a few of the little bright green leaves on the top of the wintergreen and eat them. They will also help your upset stomach." I ate the leaves and my stomach stopped hurting. All this time I was wondering how he knew about my stomach.

Then he said, "Let's go for a walk." I didn't understand at the time that this was my first encounter with my spirit guide. His name was Chitaguah (SHE tog-oo wah), but I would not learn this name or even who he was until much later in life.

As we walked along the sun-dappled paths of the forest, I noticed how the sun played off his tan skin, making little shadow stripes that ran down his arms and back, following the contours of his muscles. I looked at the ferns while he told me more things than I could ever remember about herbs. He said, "When muscles hurt from too much work, you can scrape bark from the willow, which grows in the lowland, and boil it. When the willow tea is cool enough to drink, it helps the aches. But be careful not to take too much, as it works as a blood thinner and may cause you to bleed internally."

The old Indian led me to a little meadow where red clover and a purple flower grew. About the red clover he said, "When the people's blood gets toxic, we make tea from its blossoms. To clean the blood, we drink it each morning for seven suns. This purple flower, Monarda (also known as wild bergamot), can also make a tea, a tonic for when people are sluggish and their stomachs hurt. Your mother calls this bee balm." I wondered how he knew what my mother called it.

As we walked to the low end of the small meadow, there was some black spruce growing in a small bog. Under the black spruce, on the edge of the highland, were piney-looking shrubs. They stood three to four inches tall. My parents called these princess pine.

"You make tea out of this," the old Indian said. "Also, when you are older and helping people get rid of cancer, this tea will help repair the nerves as the cancer goes away. You can also use it to help repair damaged nerves in people who have cuts or who have had surgery. And see the little buds on the birch tree? They help intensify all but a few medicines. You need to pick a supply every spring."

As we left the valley and ascended the hills, my guide told me about hundreds of herbs. He pointed out the black, tumor-looking fungus that grows on the sides of the birch trees. Later in life I would come to know it as *chaga*.

My guide said, "Chaga is a fungus that slows down, stops, or completely removes tumors." He told me that, mixed in a certain way, bearberry leaves and blueberry leaves would help out-of-balance blood sugar, as ironwood made into a tea would, also. The plant called *Sha'kel* in his language helps with depression; it is what we call St. John's Wort. And sage stem tea is a good tonic. (It is higher in vitamin C than oranges are.)

We were now moving steadily uphill between huge trees, old growth that was overlooked in the logging days of Wisconsin because the terrain was too rough to get the wood out. The lumberjacks had logged around Casey Mounds, following the Indian trails that are now runways for the white-tailed deer that live in the big woods.

Up ahead, another trail intersected the one we were on. About twenty feet from the intersection my guide stopped and asked, "What is that over there?" He was pointing to a little spot of sunshine that skewered its way through the canopy about ten feet away.

"It's a red rock; let's go look at it," I said as I started cutting across the forest floor.

"No!" he said. "You must stay on the path."

It wasn't until much later in life that the old Indian's words "stay on the path" would make sense to me. As an adult, I watched Lakota and Menominee friends of mine fall off the spiritual path—or the Red Road, as we call it. And I watched as their lives became many times harder than before.

We walked to the corner and down to the red rock. It was made of sparkling red sandstone and was about the size of a dinner plate. It might not have been quite that big, but it seemed so when I was five.

He said, "Put your hand on the rock."

"It's tingly," I said, as I did what he asked. Maybe it was the heat of the sun coming through the forest canopy, or maybe the tingling was sacred energy.

"Pick it up," said the man.

"I can't."

"How do you know? Have you tried?"

"No, but it's too big."

"Just brush away the grass and leaves from it, put your fingers around it, and try," he instructed. And so I did. I found I could pick it up, after all, because it was just a shell of rock, probably an inch and a half thick and thinner at the edges.

The man asked, "How does it feel now?"

"Hot and tingly," I answered.

He told me to turn it over. When I did so, I saw a human face on the other side. As any normal five-year-old with high hopes would have done, I hit him with the question, "Can I keep it?"

"Not now," he replied. "When you are older than me, you will have to take this to the top of the sacred hill." He pointed at a hill about four hundred feet above us.

"I'm never going to be older than you!" I said. "You are ancient." (He appeared to be about thirty-six years old.) "Why will I have to take it up there?" I asked.

"To protect the hill." he said, "Far in the future, people will ride little cars [four-wheelers] that will hurt the Earth Mother, and this rock will be good medicine for her. But for now, turn the rock over and put it back in the ground the way it was."

And so I did. I didn't know then that a sacred object like the rock was a native artifact that would confer protected status to the area where it is found. If found on the hill, in the eyes of the Department of Natural Resources (DNR) the rock would establish the hill as a sacred site to the native people. No mechanized vehicle, such as a four-wheeler, would be allowed to tear up the land.

As we continued uphill I said to the man, "The shadows are getting longer and I need to get home."

"You will," he replied. At the top of the sacred hill, he said, "Now look over here and tell me what you see."

Between the large tree trunks, in the distance I could see the sunlight glimmering off a lake. He then had me look in another direction, and another and another. I saw several distant lakes. Later in life I would learn their names as Casey, Island, Dunn, Deer, and Goose Lakes. (All of them are in the town of Casey, where I grew up.)

The man then asked me, "Do you remember how your grandmother taught you to pray?"

"Yes."

"Well, stand with your back to the center lake and reach up to the Creator as you thank him for saving you. When you are done, bring your arms down and look down your left arm, like you are aiming an arrow." The direction was south-southeast, which was exactly the direction I had to go to get home. (I wouldn't know this until I revisited the hill some ten or eleven years later, while deer hunting.)

I finished my prayer, lowered my arm, and looked out on six huge trees on six hills, which led from the hill I was standing on. I turned around to thank the old man, but he was gone. He had disappeared without a sound. I walked down the hill to the first tree; and, from there, I could see the next two trees. I walked to them, and so on. When I got to the sixth tree, I looked down and saw my dad's field. Boy, was I a happy child!

Upon returning home, I got a drink out of the water pail. My mom asked, "What have you been doing?"

"I took a little walk in the woods," I replied. Without thinking, I added in Nahuatl, the Aztec language, that I had been lost for most of the day. Then, knowing that my mother did not want me speaking that "gibberish," I quickly ran out the door.

My mother turned clear away from being native. She knew how hard it was for Native Americans living in northern Wisconsin in the 1950s, and she felt it was much safer to be proud of who you are without letting others *know* who you are. She felt that the white man had chosen to believe whatever he liked about the Native Americans. After all, everyone knew that all Indians were not only lazy but also drunks. (I am not slamming my people; that was merely the thinking in our part of the country in those days.) For this reason, I was expected to speak English at all times.

It wasn't until I was about fifteen years old that I learned about genetics in school. I learned that we natives could not drink alcohol because of something inside us. Later, I would learn that it is a defect in the DNA. Contained in our genes, DNA is like a twisted ladder with many rungs on it. Each rung of the ladder is made up of two halves joined together: one of the halves comes from your mother and the other from your father. It is these DNA segments that make us who we are. Native Americans, some northwestern Europeans such as the Finns, and other people from parts of the world where alcohol wasn't developed as early in history do not have the genetic segment that processes alcohol and refined sugar. (Alcohol is nothing more than fermented sugar.) The lack of that segment also creates a propensity for the condition known as obsessive-compulsive disorder as well as for addictions.

So, staying away from alcohol is probably the wisest choice for us. This was something I understood in the 1970s, but medical science did not figure out until the mid-'80s. I believe that early alcohol cultures probably went through the same growing pains as Native Americans are going through now. People with a genetic intolerance for alcohol probably developed diabetes as well as other alcohol-related problems and often died from overdrinking and killing too many brain cells. Their children—if they lived long enough to have children—would have been born with chronic fetal alcohol syndrome and would not have thrived, either. So, for the most part, the people without the genetic capacity to control and process sugar died off, and only people who had the segment in their DNA lived.

Nowadays, though, we have doctors who *can* keep people with alcohol intolerance alive, and those people then pass on to their children the genetic lack of ability to process sugar. Thus, we end up with people who can't control the cravings for sugar and, by the same turn, for alcohol. As we pass our genetic structure on to our children, they end up the same way we are. In essence, we Native Americans have an "on" button when it comes to drinking, but not the luxury of an "off" button.

When one parent of a child has the genetic ability to process sugar and alcohol and the other parent doesn't, 99 percent of their children will be born without the critical segment. Hence, even in cases of intermarriage between a Native American and a person of some other race, almost all the offspring will lack a tolerance for alcohol. It is no wonder, then, that people stereotype Native Americans when it comes to drinking. It is true that we have no control. But it is not anyone's fault, and it doesn't make us bad people. We just are who we are. Why would the Creator give us a genetic segment we didn't need? For most of the history of our race, processed sugar and alcohol were not available; therefore, we didn't need that gene. I am not making excuses, because we are perfect as the Creator made us. We who lack the necessary gene must be careful not to take that first drink, because, as I said, once we start, the lack of an off switch will get us every time.

I personally haven't drunk in years. It's not that I don't want to, but I know what the repercussions are. We all have to make choices. The Creator gave us free will, so he won't interfere with the trifles of man. But with the knowledge gained here, we can make better choices, and with that comes wisdom—something we could all use a little more of.

We Are All Unique

Once when I was about seven, I was walking with Gram, the snow was falling slowly, and it was cold enough that the flakes didn't melt. Gram said, "Look at the snowflakes and tell me what you see."

I looked and saw that each flake had its own distinct pattern. "They are all different; no two look alike."

"Have you ever seen two alike of *anything* the Creator God made—like trees, lakes, ponds, or even people? Everyone and everything is unique unto themselves—or itself, as the case may be. You will find the same is true of every healing, too."

"It must have taken the Creator a long time to figure everything out individually; there are a lot of things in this world," I said.

"Yes," Gram said. "Not only that, but just look at the night sky. The stars are as many as grains of sand on the beach. Yet each one is unique; they are just as individual as you are. Not many people have the gift you have, and after your Mom told me about your past-life dream a few years ago, I knew I was right about you being a healer like me."

"But, Gram, how do you know?" said I.

"Just read the signs the Creator gives you, Russell. That's how I knew about you. In the same way, you will know when the Creator brings you some other gifted one to teach. We are all different, and the Creator will choose a way just for you."

Gram Teaches Me to Walk in Love, Not Fear

It was a warm, late June day; Gram and I were digging some burdock roots out of the ground before they got their burs on. About half the sky was solid with white clouds, and the rest was spotted with clouds here and there.

A gentle breeze was softly blowing when Grandmother said, "If you are angry about something, you will find that at the core of the anger is fear. If you dislike or hate bees, it is because you don't like the pain that their stings inflict. They, however, don't hate you. They are just doing their job, protecting their nest.

"It's the same with animals and reptiles," she continued. "They are protecting themselves. So the next time something happens, before you act, ask yourself if you would walk in love. The same holds true with people. You may never know their story unless you have walked a day in their moccasins."

Another time, Gram was showing me how to gather a certain root we needed for medicine. It was one of the few root medicines she harvested, but it was plentiful. By the third root I popped out of the ground, I had how to do it down pat. I said to Gram, "Can you teach me something else? I already know how to do this."

"No, Russell. We have to get enough medicine to last the winter," she said.

"Oh pleeeeasssse, Gram! Can't we do something else?"

Gram looked around the woods we were in, and she saw water glimmering behind some trees.

"What's that?" she asked.

"What's what?"

"Look carefully through the trees and tell me what you see."

I said I noticed water sparkling on the other side of the branches.

"Good. Let's go look at it."

We walked around the trees a short way and came to a little lake. It was a hot summer day, and not a leaf or blade of grass stirred. We walked down to the shore.

"What do you see?" asked Gram.

"I see water and little squiggling things and rocks under the water, and . . . hey! I can see the water and trees and sky and a frog in the sky."

"You see a frog in the sky?"

"Yep, right there in that cloud," I said, pointing at the frog.

"You know what that is?" she asked.

"I think it is a reflection," I said.

"Honey, this is the universe. And do you know that whatever you send to the universe comes back to you amplified and magnified?"

"*Amplified*? What's that?" (We didn't have electricity in those days and so I had no idea what her words meant. At the time I was five or six. When I was fifteen I got an electric amplifier and guitar and then what she had said made more sense.)

"Look up in the sky and tell me what you see."

"Gram, I see the blue sky and the clouds, but the frog is gone."

"What about the earth?"

"I am looking in the sky," I stated.

"Okay, turn around and tell me what you see."

"I see the trees and, hey! I see the earth," I said, smiling.

"What about the lake?"

"Gram, the lake is behind us. How am I supposed to see the lake?"

"I want you to turn around slowly."

I turned around, and it hit me like a ton of bricks: By looking at the lake I could see so much more than I could see looking in any other direction.

"Gram, now I can really see everything!"

"You know, Russell, there are only two ways to walk upon the earth. You can walk in love or the opposite of love, which is . . . ?"

"Hate," I stated.

"No. You know the big cast-iron pot that I make the soup in when the relatives come over?"

"Yes."

"We are going to put all negative emotions in the pot, and we will add a little water and build a great big fire. What will happen?"

"What kind of negative emotions?"

"Oh, things like hate, rage, anger, and jealousy. As the water boils away, what would it leave?"

"It would leave a white scum on the pot."

"What is that white scum?" she asked.

"I'm not sure. Fear, maybe?"

"Yes, that scum is fear. If you boil anger down to its bare essence, you end up with fear, because there is always something we fear in whatever we're angry about. Or, if the negative emotion is jealousy, then the scum is your fear of losing or not being able to have something you want. In other words, it is your fear of lack of abundance. Does this make sense?"

"I guess. So, it's like the hoop of life? If we are mad or jealous, we are actually scared?" "You have it, basically," she affirmed.

"Thank you, Gram. I'll try to remember." I smiled.

Gram said, "As important as the lesson is to walk in love and not fear, so is the lesson of how we should be *teaching* love, not fear. As long as organized religion teaches fear and condemnation, people will be putting more fear in their heart boxes, and we will have more people to enlighten. You see, kids are taken to church, and they learn to fear instead of to love. Then they grow up and teach their kids, and the ever-growing circle perpetuates itself."

I asked, "What's per . . . par . . . pet—whatever you said?"

"It means that something reproduces itself; it replicates itself in an unending cycle. Does this make sense to you?"

"Yes, I guess so," I said. "But why doesn't the enlightenment cycle grow as fast?"

"Because when fear is taught, it is much easier for people to fall into it than to know love," Gram answered. "It is just like doing a healing: if it works, word gets around. And if it *doesn't* work, word will spread even more."

Gram was right about that. Given a chance, people will dwell on the negative most of the time. Look at the news: How many happy stories do the broadcasters report on?

Another time when I was young, Gram talked to me more about walking in love and healing work. On one of our walks she asked, "Have you ever watched a cat walking in the woods?"

"Yes," I said. "They are really smooth when they move."

"That's right, but if you watch them closely, you'll see that they always test the ground before they put their weight completely down. They lower their foot, move in a little, and then finish setting it down. It's second nature to them."

"What's 'second nature'?" I asked.

"It is like when you do something over and over until you make it look so easy that anyone thinks they can do it. Eventually, your healing will be like that: The prayers you make will continue in the back of your mind as you work on the client. While you're listening to what the Creator tells you, you'll be seeing things in your mind's eye that he shows you and drawing in his love to send to your client.

And with all that happening, at the same time you yourself will be talking—distracting the client to keep her out of her own way—so as not to block the client's own healing."

"My goodness, Grandma, do you really think I'll be able to do all those things at once?"

"Of course you will," she said, "but you will probably have a thousand or so healings under your belt by then, and that will only be a good start."

"Will I ever get that many healings done? That would take forever."

"I think that by the time you have been healing for five or six years, you will have done that many," Grandma said. "You never know where clients will come from: county fairs, hiking trails, bus stops, bars, restaurants, friends' houses, or wherever; you never know."

"Did you say *bars*?" I asked, "as in *taverns*?"

"Yes. As I said, clients might come from anywhere, and as a rule, the people in bars need a little more healing than the people in church. Not always, but sometimes."

"But, Gram, have you ever found someone to heal in a bar?"

"Yes," she said, "I know you don't drink, but there's no rule that you have to drink when you go to a bar. They sell pop, ya know. And I don't go there to find clients. I go there to allow clients to find me. You see?"

"I think so; we have to go places so people can find us?"

"More or less. If you're not out there, how will they find you? You will need to act in such a way that your client base is continually growing. As you heal one, they tell two. As you heal two, they tell four, and so on.

"Someday you will be so busy you will have to schedule time for yourself. We have relatives in Ontario, so that would be a good place to go when you want to relax, because other people don't know you there. But don't think you'll go unnoticed for long. Healers attract people without trying. People who need your help will find you no matter where you are, so it's something you have to get used to. Also, being a healer is hard on relationships."

"What kind of 'ships'?" I asked.

"Relationships—your mates or wives when you marry. Healing is a selfless job. Doing the Creator's work takes its toll on families. First, there is the attraction: if you are a male, female clients will be attracted to you, just as men will be to a woman healer. Part of the attraction is that everyone tries to put us healers on pedestals, where we don't belong. It's the Creator who does the healing, and he alone should get the credit. But many clients will give you the credit instead and want to be with you. So can you see how that would be hard on your marriage? If you were old and married and women were trying to pick you up, can you understand how a wife would feel?"

"You mean like when I'm thirty years old?" I asked. "I guess so, but if we walk in truth and love, there would be nothing to worry about, right?"

"In theory, that is correct, but hugging is part of healing, and some people are not as understanding as healers. In reality, if everyone walked in love, there would be no jealousy. And that's because jealousy is based in—what?"

"Fear, right?"

"Totally correct," she said. "Why?"

"Because there are only two bases—love and fear—and if something is not about love, it has to be about fear."

"Good!" she said. "You are learning well, so keep up the good work. It will help you to teach later in life."

I said, "I don't want to be a teacher. I only like half of the teachers I have, so I wouldn't want to be one."

"There will come a time when you won't have a choice, because it will just happen as a side effect. You won't be deliberately teaching; it will simply be happening as you talk. So just let it flow and don't worry about teaching or not teaching, because it doesn't matter. Worry doesn't change anything. Life is what it is.

"Cool," I said.

"As you go through life, you'll notice there seem to be two things that program and rule most people: food and propagation. But if you walk in love, everything else comes of its own accord through the Creator."

Energy Exchange

When I was eight years old, once when Gram was gathering herbs she and I talked about energy in healing. She said, "For healing to take place, there needs to be an energy exchange. It is alright if people want to make a donation, but the donation is not about the money. It is about showing the Creator that people really want and need the healing. A healer uses energy to help people, and they need to show that they have some energy to exchange for what the healer does for them," she said.

"You need to start feeling the energy of things," Grandma went on, holding out a plant she had just picked. "Can you feel the energy in this?"

"Yes," I said.

"Good! You know, when I do a healing, I sense the energy of the person, and that shows me what I need to do. It will be years before you will be able to see things like I do, but you will."

Grandma was right. It took time to develop sensitivity to the flow of energy in my clients. When I first began healing, I had to start by feeling the energy from the person. I would find a spot on the client's body and ask him what I was feeling, and he would usually tell me (if he knew). I would store this information in a little drawer in a room in my mind.

This mental room is much like that of a post office. It is full of little boxes, each one representing a past healing I have done. My ability to use these boxes is a gift from the Creator. It is the gift of seeing images and organizing them, which assists me in my work. Thus, whenever I need information about a client or a disease, I can go directly into the correct box. How I know which box to go to is beyond me. I find it amazing that this is so simple. Once I'm in the right box, I am able to compare the energy I feel with a new client to the energy I felt with a former one. Needless to say, this system is quite helpful for doing long-distance healings, too.

"Did your mom have you feel her energy?" I asked Gram.

"No," she replied, "but she told me about the light and the energy and explained it to me. Just as I am teaching you, my mother taught me to start by working on small critters such as birds, dogs, and cats. A healer draws in God's energy, in the form of light. It is passed through your arms, then to the people or critters that come to you.

"You must not choose who to heal," she cautioned. "Those who are supposed to come to you will come, be it beast or man. It has always been this way; it was in the time of my grandmothers, and it will continue to be as long as there is healing. If some people don't show up for their healings, don't take offense; just know that the time is not right for them."

A Missionary's Disturbing Message

One July day in 1959, I decided to stay home and play outside while my dad took the rest of the kids to town. A brand-new car pulled into our driveway. Accustomed as we were to our 1950 Chevy Biscayne four-door coupè, this car was impressive.

A man got out of the car and asked, "Your mom and dad home?"

"No," I answered.

He said, "I am a missionary, and I teach people about Jesus's love. Would you like for me to talk to you about Jesus?"

"I know about Jesus!" I eagerly replied.

"What do you know?"

"I know he was a master healer and teacher and that he was about peace and love."

"Where did you learn that?"

"My Indian grandmother," I said proudly.

"Do you go to church?" the man asked, narrowing his eyes.

"No; my grandmother is a healer and she says our church is anywhere we are and that you don't have to be in a building to pray to God."

"Your grandmother is a witch and a heathen! You both are going to hell!" The man was very passionate and almost yelling. "You can't get to heaven without Jesus," he went on, "and God will send you to hell to burn forever!"

"How can that happen?" I asked, sort of scared.

"Because that's the way God does it," he declared. "Are you baptized?"

"What's that?" I asked.

"That is where your sins are washed away."

"I ain't got no sin."

"Oh, yes you do!" the man yelled. "You were born with it."

"I got it from my mom?"

"No, my child, you got it from Eve."

"I don't even *know* Eve; how could I catch it from her?"

"Because she ate from the Tree of Knowledge," the man explained.

"Was she an Indian, too?" I asked.

"Why, no, she was white."

"How do you know?"

"It says so in the Bible."

"Did God write the Bible?"

"No, it was written by men who were told by God what to say." The man leaned into the open window of his car and brought out a Bible.

I continued with my questions. "So, you have this Bible; it must be really old."

He said, "It's not the original. It is a copy, and I have one for you, too."

I snapped back with, "I don't want a copy. I want the original."

"You can't read the original."

"Why not?"

"Because," the man said, "it was written in ancient Hebrew."

"What is that?"

"Well, it's Jewish."

"So, are you telling me Jesus was a Jew?"

"NO!" The man was yelling again.

"Where was Jesus from?" I asked.

"Jerusalem or Nazareth."

"He sounds Jewish to me."

"No! Jesus was a Christian!" he said, yelling some more. He was very adamant about his beliefs.

I couldn't help but ask, "How come the Bible was written in Jewish, then? Couldn't anybody write in white back then?"

Sounding frustrated, the man said, "Listen, why don't you come to Bible study at Sunday school and bring a tithe."

"Okay, but what does a tithe look like, so if I see one, I can catch it and bring it for you?"

"A tithe," he said, "is a contribution."

"A *contribution*?"

"You know, money."

"How come your God needs money?" I asked. "Our Creator only wants our love."

Not letting up, the man asked, "Have you been saved by Jesus so that you won't burn in hell forever?"

"No," I replied. "I guess I should be, because that sounds scary, that hell thing you keep talking about. What do I have to do?" I asked.

"Pray with me," he urged.

Thus began my confusion about Christianity. I went to Bible study and attended church when I could. It served me well until, during my second or third month in Vietnam, I listened to a Christian chaplain on a hill one Sunday. He gave a beautiful sermon about love and peace. But when he finished, he said, "Be careful out there! And by the way, boys, I've blessed your weapons. So get out there and kill those Commie bastards."

Jesus was about love, peace, and honor. Needless to say, I was confused about how the chaplain's hateful words fit with those teachings.

When I was a child, the missionary said to me, "Now that you are saved by Jesus, you have to stay away from your witch grandmother."

I did stay away from Gram somewhat, but not always, of course. When I did see her, I wouldn't tell the man. I continued my education with her, but you could never imagine the turmoil that caused in my young life.

"Where have you been?" asked Grandma.

"Oh, I have been busy."

"What's bothering you?"

I started to tear up. "The missionary man said you were a witch."

"Well, don't you worry about it! You know the truth."

I listened carefully as Gram said, "There were no witches here before the Europeans landed. If he says we do voodoo, you tell him he missed history class when he went to school, because there wasn't any voodoo here until the Europeans brought slaves to work the plantations.

"Remember, a lot of people will fear you in life because of the things you say and teach and, especially, because of the healing you can do. Remember, when people fear you, they feel trapped. You shouldn't listen to what they say, even if they try to bully you. They can hurt you with words only *if you choose to let them*. So, it is your choice: whether to listen and be hurt, or to ignore them and let go of the words like water runs off a duck's back."

That teaching reminds me of another one Gram gave me a couple of years later. As she and I were talking one fall day in 1961, she asked, "Russell, you know how, whenever we run into people who need help and ask for it, it is up to us to do our best to help them? That's all the Creator expects from us. Just do the best you can, and it will be good enough in the spiral of life."

As my grandmother taught me, the spirit land, unlike the Christian heaven, is a whole series of plateaus in an ever-upward spiral. A river flows down each side to a waterfall that drops to the next-lower plateau, over and over again. The spirit land is where we go to rest and to study the lifetime we just finished. We go there to see if we learned our lessons and to determine which lessons we need for the next life. After we have rested for as long as we need, then we get ready to come back.

Gram said, "In the spirit land, we get to see our physical families and our soul families. After we rest and are ready to come back, our guides help us figure out which families to choose in order to receive the necessary lessons. Why would we do this? Through learning our lessons in each lifetime, we can eventually attain enlightenment, after which we can choose whether or not to come back to earth again. We might become guides in the spirit land or on earth, so that we may teach lessons to others."

In my own healing work now, I find that some of my clients' problems may, in fact, be coming not from this life but from past lives. It seems these people have issues that follow them from life to life because they haven't ever dealt with them. If you are such a person, it will be useful for you to find someone to help you deal with your past-life problems. You'll be better off!

You can't stand in the way of yourself, because if you do, you will get run over! All the Creator wants from us is for us to learn our lessons so that we can move up the spiral of life. But the journey is not guaranteed to be one-way. If we are stubborn—if we refuse to recognize the lessons when they are presented or even ignore them when we do see them—we can go down the spiral. If you learn your lessons, you will head up the spiral toward final attainment; but if you don't, the very least that will happen is that, in the next life, you will have the same kind of life you had in this one. The worst possible scenario is that you slip down the spiral and come back in a life that is many times worse than your present one. Do you really want a harder life than the one you have now? I know I don't. It has been a doozy this time, so, at least on my part, I want a better life next time.

How do we slip? As I said, we can ignore our lessons. Worse yet, we can fail to speak our truth; we can *lie* to people. Knowing an answer and not speaking it is the same as lying. If we see a problem and don't talk about it, does it go away? Of course not. At some level, we all are responsible for what is going on in the United States right now. We refuse to use our power when we let someone else do the voting for us. Roughly half the people don't use their voices in a presidential race and even more don't in other elections. If we don't use our voices and make the effort to vote, then we have no reason to complain about the state of things.

The only hell is here in the physical realm! A cousin of mine, Ren, was a bad man in his younger years—drug dealer, drunkard, always hurting people who were late paying him for the drugs he sold them. His life got so bad that, when he was thirty-five, he shot and killed a man and ended up in the Stillwater penitentiary. Within three months, he was running all the dope going out of or coming into the prison. After he had served half of his sentence, he started shooting up the drugs he was controlling and got hepatitis C from a dirty needle. Then he found God and turned himself completely around. He attended church regularly, never missed a Sunday service, quit all drugs, and gave himself to God. He spent his last four years in jail as a model prisoner, and the warden dropped two years off his sentence.

After he got out, Ren volunteered at my healing center, taking phone calls, making appointments, and so on. We had a lot of time to talk while we rode back and forth to the center. I found he had signed for a very rough life this time around. On one of our drives, he said, "You know, I'm going to hell."

"Why?" I asked.

"Well, according to the church, I have committed five of the seven deadly sins that can't be forgiven."

"Are you nuts?"

"Well, that's what the reverend said."

"Ren, there is no hell."

"What do you mean?"

"We are not here for just one life; we come back many, many times." I went on to explain Gram's teaching about the purpose of each life being to learn certain lessons, and, if we do, we move up the spiral. I told Ren about going to the spirit land when we die, where our personal guides help us study the lessons we got and didn't get. They also help us figure out which family to be born into next in order to get the lessons we still need and the ones we should have already learned but didn't. And I told him about the waterfall in the spirit land falling from one level to another: when it is time to be reborn, we wade out into the river and drink from it as we cross.

"The water is sweet," I said, "and, as a rule, we drink our fill, and this helps us. When we get to the far edge, we step from the river into the particular bag of water from which we are going to be born."

Ren wondered how I knew all this, and I told him that, the last time I was getting ready to come back, when I was crossing the river I wasn't very thirsty. The name of the river is the River of Forgetfulness. Because I hadn't drunk much from it, when I came back I remembered my past lives and what went on in the spirit land. I also remembered some of the choices I had made in my former life, and that got me into trouble. Ren asked why. "Because this is a completely different life from the last one," I said. "The choices I made then don't work in this one. They become bad choices now."

"Well, if you are right, then when I die I will find a way to contact you," Ren said.

Now, as things go, Ren's liver went bad, and when he was sixty-five he crossed to the spirit land. I figured that he would come to me in a vision, but not the way that he did.

Three months after Ren died, I got a voice-mail message from Sedona on my cell phone. The phone didn't actually ring, but it did display a number, and that is how my son figured out where the message came from. Oddly enough, it had been sent from a direct-line fax machine in a doctor's office in Modesto, California, to a fax machine in a medical transcriptionist office in Sedona. How it had arrived on my cell phone is beyond me! But I let more than fifty of my clients hear the message—and that was perfectly clear: Ren sang a little song to me that he used to sing after he'd had four or five beers. "Tada da, tada da!" Then he sang, "Love you, brother. You are right; it's nice here." And at the end of the song, he said, "This is Ren, if you don't recognize me."

I let my niece listen to the message without telling her what it was. As she listened, she started to cry, saying, "That's cousin Ren! How long ago did he send that to you?"

"Yesterday."

"But he's been dead for three months! Why did his message take so long to arrive?"

"Listen again to what he is saying," I replied. She was shocked when Ren said it was nice there.

I got the brilliant idea to record Ren's voice, so I bought a Dictaphone and a new tape and turned on the recorded message. All I got was white noise. I figure that Ren didn't want me to record it. Then, on the one-year anniversary of the phone call, another message appeared on my phone. Again, no rings; just the message:

"Hi, this is Ren. Just want you to know you are right. This is the most beautiful place ever. Mom and Dad say hi, and they will be seeing you." I didn't even try to record the message this time but had a lot of people, including my niece, listen to it again and again.

After thinking for many years about this lesson, I wondered about newborn babies who live an hour or a week and then die. What lesson did such a short life hold for them? Then the answer came to me: They didn't need any lessons, because they must have already reached attainment. Instead of having been born this time to learn lessons, they must have come to teach a lesson to someone else—most likely someone who knew them but, in some cases, society as a whole.

I have also wondered about murder victims. Either the victim or the perpetrator may have a lesson they need to learn. But even perpetrators can teach society lessons in terms of the consequences of collectively failing to help sick or mentally ill people.

When we see others being wronged and do nothing about it, aren't we, as part of the social body, as responsible as the government? If more of us would give freely of ourselves to help those in need, the world would be a better place for us all. It is common to think that someone else will do the work and we need only to wait; but the time for waiting is over. What we need now is action—opening that door, for instance, when someone's hands are full of groceries. Everyone has, at some time, hurried by an elder in need instead of pausing the ten or fifteen seconds it would have taken to open a door for that person. I am off to Couchiching Reserve in Ontario to do some hunting for the elders who can't get out for themselves. Do I get money for doing this? No; I just get the satisfaction of knowing I have helped several old people make it through another cold Canadian winter. Doing such things gives you the warm fuzzies, if you allow yourself to feel them.

I am concerned that the younger generation of indigenous people hasn't stepped up to the plate yet to help their elders, as was done in the old days. Is it their fault? No! When the United States and Canada assimilated the native population, they sent the majority of the people to boarding schools to make model citizens out of them. And they did a good job of it! They got rid of a culture that had served the people in conglomerate for hundreds of thousands of years. It worked like this: elders were not stuck in nursing homes and forgotten about; their every want and need was met by the youngsters of the tribe, out of respect. This respect largely vanished during the assimilation, as a whirlwind on the prairie does when it runs out of energy. It might reappear now and again, but for the most part, it is just gone.

One medicine man I knew died without having had any apprentices, and it is with deep humility that I grieve his loss. Almost all the elder medicine men can't find apprentices because the young don't want to learn any more. When these elders die, their medicine dies with them. Sadly, we can't find enough young people who are interested in what has always been a big part of their culture. I sincerely hope this state of affairs changes while there is still time. It is what happens to a culture when the respect for it and its customs are lost. I suppose it is a form of evolution, sad though it is.

Gram Gets Serious

Although Gram and I had touched on the subject of the army and the war in Vietnam in the past, one day in 1968, when I was a junior in high school, she said, "Lots of boys are getting killed in Vietnam. If you get drafted next year after you graduate, I want you to promise that you will take your training seriously. Learn everything your teachers teach you, because most of them will have been there and know what to expect. So please, promise me you will, okay?"

"Sure, Grandma, I'll do the best I can," I said.

"When you get there, you'll meet other Indian boys. Stick with them, because they will know the right way to be. You will find a lot of prejudice in the service, and you will be in a bad place. The blacks will think you are white, the whites will call you Indian, and you will be stuck in the middle. I'm sure you will make friends. Remember always to walk in love, and you'll have a much easier time than some of the boys will. You grew up in the woods, but most of the people you'll meet will have grown up in the city."

"Why do you think that?"

"Well, more boys *live* in the city than in the country, so it stands to reason that more will be drafted from the city. If you have a hundred thousand boys in Chicago and fifty in Spooner, how likely are you to end up with someone from Spooner?"

"I see your point."

"When they ask you what's going on, speak your truth. Tell them about walking in love instead of fear; you know the idea well enough by now to pass it on."

"I'll do my best, Gram."

"I sure am glad the signs showed up when you were a baby."

"What signs?"

"You know, the dream you had about your grandfather and the conquistadors," Gram answered. "Mark my words: when you are older, you will train others to be healers, but you'll be lucky to find one individual who will be nearly as gifted as you are."

"I'm not sure what you mean."

"In my whole life—which is considerable—I have never met a person with a gift like yours. I trained a few when I was younger, but no one had the connection to spirit you have."

"Oh, Gram, you're just saying that to make me feel good."

"No, I am truly grateful that the Creator and your guides brought you to my family; my grandmother felt the same when she found me. So, when you finally find that young person who is like you, be grateful, too. You won't know what I'm talking about until then, but one day he will come along."

"How will I recognize him, Gram?"

"When you are older, you will find that you just do," she assured me. "And when it happens, remember what we've talked about."

"Okay, I'll try."

"No, there is no 'try'; there is only 'do' or 'not do,' remember?"

"Yes, I remember, and I will."

"There is always a chance that you won't get drafted, but since they're looking at almost all the people of draft age, don't count on it. When you take their test, do the best you can, okay? It may help you get a better job than carrying a rifle."

"To tell you the truth, Gram, I like hunting, and I think I would rather carry a rifle than be stuck in some office somewhere," I replied.

"Well, if you do the best you can, it will be good enough, and maybe you will gain a little control. But don't go overboard with it, because it will come back to haunt you. Control equates to power, and power can go to people's heads. So pay attention to what you are doing."

"I will, Gram. I know who is in charge."

"Good! You are a good boy, and I know that you will stay on the light side as much as possible," she said.

"You know I will," I promised.

Vietnam, 1970

In 1970, at the age of eighteen I did find myself in the US Army. We were told that communism was spreading around the world; and, as a native person, I thought I might do my part in keeping America free. One of the ways native people can truly be warriors is by counting coups, and the Vietnam War presented a situation where that could be done. Counting coups is like an honor system in which one earns eagle feathers for bravery. In traditional native culture, one of the lower forms of counting coups was to be the first to touch a dead enemy. Maybe ten of those coups would earn you a feather. Another way was to kill an enemy; maybe two of those would get you a feather. Another way was to touch a *living* enemy. That might have gained you a feather, but if you touched a living enemy and disarmed him, that could have been worth a feather and a half.

So counting coups awarded more points for touching an enemy than for killing him outright. *Touching* brought much more honor than just *killing*. Killing someone could be done at a distance with a bow; it was a far more courageous thing to disarm him and send him home in defeat.

When I was first sent for training to Fort Jackson, South Carolina, the heat was like nothing I had ever experienced. I had thought Wisconsin was hot and muggy. But *nnnooo*, I was mistaken. Swampy South Carolina was much, much muggier. But even South Carolina was nothing compared to what I was headed for.

By the early fall of 1970, when I was nineteen, I was stationed in Vietnam, ten or eleven thousand miles from home. And I was afraid, to say the least—maybe even petrified. I expected to get shot instantly, as soon as I got off the plane and hit the tarmac. But that didn't happen. The airport where I landed was well guarded. It was in the city of Bien Hoa (Ben WAH), just north of Saigon.

As we got off the plane, the hairs on my neck stood up. It didn't help that in boot camp the guys coming back from 'Nam had always been telling us stories of how bad it was seeing all the blood and guts. You can understand why eighteen- and nineteen-year-olds would be frightened. The air smelled of all sorts of odors I didn't recognize. I soon discovered that I could do something I had never before realized I could do: I could separate smells. I knew the difference between the smell of the heat, the smell of diesel, and the odor of the latrines. It wasn't that I actually wanted this ability; it just happened. And boy, that stench was something to experience.

Adding to the unusual variety of aromas was the unmistakable scent of burning crap. Ironically, this was the military's sanitary measure. And there was another, peculiar odor—a far-away, indiscernible scent that would waft in the wind sometimes as the currents eddied around the airport. It was a while before I figured out what it was. It was the smell of death. I instinctively didn't like it, even though I had never come across the scent before. The smell of dead humans is a scent I can never forget, as if it is burned into my brain. To this day, I can recognize the smell of a dead body at a hundred meters, as could any soldier who was in Vietnam.

I would rather have been doing many other things than wading through rice paddies while carrying a rucksack that outweighed me by forty or fifty pounds. However, I believe the Creator had a purpose in sending me there, though it would be many years before I would understand it. For me, the purpose was to get comfortable with death, so that when I eventually had clients with stage-four cancer or some other devastating disease, I would not fear them but be able to help; and I would know that, in reality, the outcome is truly in the Creator's hands.

On my first day in Vietnam, after landing at the Bien Hoa air base our group of 120 soldiers was sent off by helicopter to booby-trap school. I was excited about my first helicopter ride. I was also worried and scared, all at the same time. It was like my first trip to town as a small child.

Not long after lifting off, we took some fire from somewhere on the ground outside the perimeter. I didn't recognize the rat-tat-tat as machine-gun fire until I saw a three-foot piece of the main rotor that kept us in the air fly off and disappear below us. Then I realized that I had to be on my toes, no matter what the circumstance. The helicopter began wobbling back and forth and twirling and vibrating horribly as it plummeted toward the ground. At that moment, I was sure I was a dead man. It's funny that, in such situations, the Creator puts everything in slow motion: it was in slow motion that I saw the end of the rotor make its revolutions away from the helicopter as it dropped. I remember thinking, "Damn! First day in the country, and I get killed before I've even seen an enemy!" Many of the new guys were screaming about dying. We managed to land, more or less safely, but it is surprising how quickly a chopper can fall a couple hundred feet. It's also amazing how much fear you can pack into a couple hundred feet when you are completely out of control and can do nothing to change the situation.

With the helicopter out of commission, along with a hundred other newbies I was sent by truck convoy up to Cam Ranh Bay, where the booby-trap school was. As we traveled, we passed through several little villages. The Vietnamese didn't have chairs; their habit was to sit on their haunches. We would see groups of three or four men or women sitting that way, always separate, never together. In

one village, I smelled burning weeds or grass. I asked the guy next
to me what that smell was.

"You don't know?"

"No; it smells like burning grass fields, like we have back in
Wisconsin."

"It's grass, alright, but not like you burned at home. It's pot,
dummy!"

"Well, I never smelled it before."

The booby-trap school usually lasted two to three hours a day.
For the rest of the time, the sergeant gave us various keep-busy jobs,
such as policing the grounds and guarding the camp. The moment
came when, out of the hundred soldiers, all but seven had been
assigned duties. One of the only jobs left was burning the crap from
the outhouses. Obviously, I was relieved when an engineer asked if
anybody knew how to weld. I did know how and gladly volunteered
for that job, not wanting to burn crap!

The engineer led me to the back of an airport hangar where there
were many colorful, orange-and-white-striped barrels and a cutting
torch. He told me to cut a few hundred of the barrels in half; with
wooden seats placed on the upright, open ends of them, they would
become toilets. After I had cut the barrels, I was to make a hole near
the top of each half. The hole was for transporting the toilet, which
was done with a piece of reinforcing rod that had a handle on one
end and was bent into a hook on the other. By inserting the hook
into the hole at the top of the barrel, you could stay a few feet away
from the full toilets as you dragged them from the outhouses.

Some of the barrels were labeled "2,4-D"; "Agent Purple"; "Agent
White"; "Agent Blue"; and "2,4,5-T." All were types of Agent Orange-
like substances, although, according to the US government, none of
these agents were ever used in Vietnam!

"Won't the oil in those barrels be bad to breathe?" I asked.

"No, they have all been rinsed, so it won't hurt you," came the reply.

The engineer then handed me a pair of sunglasses so dirty I couldn't see out of them and said, "I'll be back to get you at the end of the day."

I commenced cutting the barrels in half and making crappers out of them. By the time I had fifty of them done, my lungs felt like they were on fire. But a job is a job, I reminded myself, and at least I am not burning crap. I ended up with a cold in my chest that lasted for three weeks. When I got to the field, the men complained about all the coughing I was doing.

I still thought I had gotten the better end of the deal until I returned home on leave from Vietnam and started falling down. Unbeknownst to me, the barrels had indeed been containers for Agent Orange. Cutting the barrels in half with the acetylene torch had exposed me to smoke from the burning chemical. Besides falling down, I also developed other major health problems, including nerve damage, rashes, and, later, various types of cancers. However, *none* of these problems—according to the VA—were caused by the Agent Orange. Right on! How very fortunate for me! Some of the nerves in my back are paralyzed, and I have lost a bit of feeling; but, through healing and herbal teas, I have almost completely recovered.

After booby-trap school was over, we traded our stateside uniforms for jungle fatigues, boots, and an empty rucksack and were assigned a unit. I was going to Chu Lai, up north, where I would be in the Second Platoon Charlie Company, Second Battalion, First Infantry, 196th brigade—or, as we wrote it, *C-2d/1st Inf. 196th Bde. Americal RVN* (Republic of Vietnam).

At that time in 1970, the commanders of my division, called the "Americal" (23th Infantry), sent platoons, typically consisting of fifteen to thirty men, to the field to work as a single unit. A full platoon was actually twenty-eight to thirty guys, but I don't recall there ever being more than twenty-five.

The other platoons were as much as a mile or two away. I'm thinking that this was not one of the better ideas to come from the big experiment called the Vietnam War. The platoons being stationed so far apart made us easy targets for the Viet Cong. At one point, in our platoon we had only seven or eight men left, the rest having been wounded or killed in action.

Once the enemy located a platoon, it was easy for them to harass it constantly. When we were moving on foot, they would get ahead of us and set booby traps. When we settled in for some sleep, they would situate themselves on two or three sides of the camp and fire a clip or two of ammo. (There went your sleep for the rest of the night.)

The conditions made for unbearable stress. I learned to sleep with one eye open so that no VC could slip up on me. In training, before I went to 'Nam, I had heard about this style of sleeping and didn't really think it could be true. But it was, and I mastered it with a little practice. If someone walked in front of my tent while I was sleeping, I would find myself sitting up with my weapon changed from safe to full automatic before I was fully awake. Who would have thought that possible? It is amazing what you can adapt to when your life depends on it.

One day at Chu Lai the battalion commander told me to get on a chopper taking mail out and to be careful, as we were going to a hot "LZ," or landing zone. We went into it with machine guns blazing the wood line around where the purple smoke wafted up through the trees. I thought the smoke was a good sign, as, in the native way, purple is the color of healing. When we landed, men ran up to the chopper for mail and C-rats, and four guys brought a large, black, heavy bag. At first I didn't know what it was, but I soon figured out that it was a body bag; no one had to tell me. I thought, what kind of a messed-up place did I come to, for Christ's sake?

At that point I got off the chopper. After it left, a sergeant named Draves showed me how to fill my new rucksack. A couple of the more seasoned guys chimed in and said that I might want to take this or that. One gave me a machine-gun belt, and others gave me things, too. In fact, when they were finished sharing, I couldn't get the pack off the ground. Then Sergeant Draves came over and said, "All you wise guys take your equipment back." The older men said they had just been spoofing me. But I was never sure what was supposed to be a joke and what wasn't, since my first days in 'Nam were a blur while I was trying to learn what was going on.

Most of the "older" men—and I am not talking chronologically; I am talking guys who were still alive after six months—didn't want much to do with the "cherries," as they called us newcomers. I guess they didn't want to get to know you unless they were sure you would hold up in battle and not get them killed. After my fourth day there, our RTO (radio telegraph operator) got hit, and Sergeant Stailey asked if I would carry the radio. I did carry the radio for a month or so, until I decided I wanted a little more excitement and asked if there was something else I could do.

"Jamaica is going home in a couple weeks," said the sergeant. "You want to walk point?" *Walking point* means being the first guy in a line of men; out there in front, you watch for ambushes, trip wires, punji traps, land mines, and poisonous snakes.

"Sure," I said, "I would love to be up there."

So for the next two weeks, as Jamaica got ready to leave, he told me all about walking point: "You take your eyes as you are walking. Look up the left side of the trail, and, when you are as far as you can safely see, scan back down the right side. Then scan up the middle of the trail. Then down the left side and back up the right. That way, you hit every piece of trail four times from different directions."

Once I got the hang of it, I found that Jamaica's instructions fit right in with what my gram had taught me. But the first day I walked point alone, I was just a bit apprehensive. And that night, Gram came to me in a vision or a dream. She reminded me that I should walk in love rather than fear.

"Gram, you know that the VC are using real bullets, and they are trying to kill me," I protested.

"Yes, but who is in charge of how long we live?" she asked.

"Well, the Creator is."

"That is right. Now let's say that next Thursday, a week from today, at three o'clock in the afternoon, your number is up, and you will be going to the spirit land to be with the Creator. What are you going to do? Count the grains of sand as they slide down the hourglass for the next seven days? Or enjoy the time you have left?"

"I think I will enjoy the time I have left, because I have had enough fear to last me a lifetime." Then, as an afterthought, I asked, "Am I going to die?"—thinking, in my nineteen-year-old mind, that Gram knew something I didn't.

"How would I know that?" she asked.

"I was just wondering, since you said that thing about next week."

"You know that only the Creator knows the time when someone is going back to the spirit land. And we don't live one minute longer (or less) than the Creator gives us, so there is no use in worrying about it, because it won't change anything. Putting worry in your heart box affects only you, and you will be the one who ends up with an ulcer because of the energy you have stolen from your own body."

That we have a heart box is one of the most important healing lessons my gram taught me. Earlier in this book, I explained that the heart box is the void between our hearts, our spines, and our lungs where we store hurts and traumas. I also shared the ways Gram taught me to unburden the heart box.

When Gram came to my dreams again, I asked, "If I were to walk in love, would it make things better in this armpit of the world?"

"This is a beautiful place," she replied. "You just have to open your eyes to the beauty and see what is before you. Take away the bomb craters, and the jungle is pretty. Remember the things I taught you when we went to the woods to gather plants for medicine work. Notice everything. The animals will let you know when something is wrong. Move through the trees as I taught you: hold your breath, so that if an enemy steps on a twig, you will be able to hear it. This may save your life one day."

Gram went on, "But as I said, don't worry about dying, as it will turn out however the Creator wants it. Never kill an enemy out of anger, only in self-defense, and send him home with love. He won't die unless the Creator wants him. Remember who's in charge and who will always be in charge, as you walk the point. I gotta go now."

I awoke with a start and settled back to listening to the crickets and the croaking tree frogs. I was glad I wasn't the one doing the croaking.

The morning after the vision about Gram, I walked point again. Now walking in love, I was able to move at a much faster pace than when I had been walking in fear. In fact, the sergeant sent word to ease up a little; and, by noon break, he came over to me.

"Who the hell set a blaze under your saddle?" he asked.

"No one set a blaze, why?" I replied.

"You are getting too far out front, and the guys are afraid that you are going to miss something."

"You don't have to worry about my missing anything, because I'll use my Indian skills to find them."

"Right. Just be careful," he responded.

I had taken my gram's words to heart about walking point in love and not fear. But, truthfully, I couldn't tell whether things worked better that way, because I hadn't found any booby traps yet.

"Tell the guys not to walk in fear," I innocently told the sergeant.

"What the hell does that mean?"

"Oh, nothing," I answered, guessing that he had probably never had a healer for a grandmother.

After the noon meal, I got the word to move out. I hadn't walked two hundred yards before I saw a trip wire going across the path and called a halt. Oddly enough, I saw the trip wire from more than fifty feet away. It looked as thick as a pencil. In reality, the trip wires were painted camouflage green and were as thin as pencil lead.

"Hey, Tiny! Look there," I said to my machine gunner, pointing up the trail.

"Look where?" he asked.

"Right up there. Don't you see it?" I insisted.

"See what? What the hell are you talking about?"

"It's a trip wire going across the trail."

"Russell, I think you are seeing things. There is no trip wire on this trail," he replied.

"Come with me," I said. We walked about forty feet closer. "Do you see it now?"

"Well, I'll be going to hell. How did you see that way back there?" Tiny asked in disbelief.

"Tiny, it looked as big as a clothes-line rope to me!" It made me happy to think that what Gram had said was—as always—true. Hey, I thought, this walking in love sure takes some of the work out of walking point! After Tiny and I blew up the booby trap, we continued on.

Further up the trail, I was walking at a fast clip when the hairs on the back of my neck started standing at attention, like so many little soldiers. I called a halt again. Ever so slowly, I moved one leaf at a time to see what I could find.

It was a homemade landmine made of a fifty-one-caliber bullet inside pieces of bamboo and buried so that just the tip of the bullet poked out of the ground. A nail that was cut off flush with the node at the bottom was driven through the node so that, if someone stepped on it with full weight, the nail would pierce the primer, send the bullet up through your leg, and leave your body through the top of your shoulder. I looked further and found six more of these fiendish devices at various spots on the trail. You had to give the Viet Cong credit. Resourceful and industrious, they could make booby traps out of nothing. These devices were more than adequate to kill a guy or wound him, terribly.

That experience was particularly hair-raising, but there was no time in Vietnam that I ever felt safe. It was twenty-four hours a day, seven days a week of nonstop adrenalin surges. In ordinary life, the adrenal glands are half the size of a little fingernail, and that gives a person all he needs for the fight-or-flight mechanism in our bodies. But in the extremely dangerous conditions of war, the need for fight or flight triggers a surge of adrenalin ten times a day, and the adrenal glands grow bigger so as not to work so hard. The bigger they grow, the more adrenalin they produce, and the more on edge you always feel.

Nevertheless, as the weeks went by, I became more and more comfortable practicing walking in love. Soon the other point-men wanted to know what I had, or was doing, because no one ever got hurt following me on my platoon's day to do the hump (go on some kind of patrol).

We came close one day, though. I was walking point, and the trail came to a river that was shallow and running through rocks, so it was all whitewater. I couldn't see the bottom, so I walked upstream to where the water was a little slower and just a bit deeper, and walked across there. In the meantime, the platoon sergeant had waded out into the whitewater directly from the trail and was hurrying the guys to cross the river in front of him, just like John Wayne in one of his war movies. After the last man crossed, the sergeant himself began crossing the river at the trail point. Looking back, I saw him jerk his foot out of the water just as a tiger trap snapped shut. The trap was about sixteen inches across and had half-inch teeth that crossed when it closed. The sergeant didn't get caught, but it cut the sole of his boot off. So he limped the rest of the way across the river, and we stopped so that he could put on one of his extra boots. "Way to go, John Wayne!" I said to him as we were laughing.

"At least I felt the trap pan go when I stepped on it. I tried to take my sole out, and you would have needed a C clamp to open the damn thing," he said, still laughing.

Another time in Vietnam, I was sitting on a hill in our night defensive position, and the Viet Cong sent some rocket-propelled grenades (RPGs) at us. It was getting dark, and the RPGs fell short, landing on top of another grassy hill five to six hundred feet shorter than the one we were on. They hit in the middle of the lower hill, and it was the dry season. A small fire started, progressing slowly, as, even in the dry season, it was dewy at night. After a half hour, the fire started moving down the side of the hill. As I watched, it made a ring. A burning ring, a ring of fire, and—son of a gun if I didn't get Johnny Cash's song in my head! Again I thought of Gram's words, "What do you do if the world gives you a basket of lemons?" I enjoyed the "lemonade" of that song for the rest of the night.

Gram showed me that you could survive most anything with the Creator as your guide. Her advice served me very well, even in South Vietnam. I never hated the enemy, because I knew they were just trying to defend what they considered their home. Who does it hurt when we hate? Not the *other* person, now, does it?

Bonsai Charge!

In March of 1971, we had just closed down Khe Sanh and come in for a stand-down at Camp Perdue in Da Nang. It was our relief time. It felt good to be out of the stress of battle. For the three or four days we had off, we could eat, drink, or smoke anything we wanted. We could eat steaks, shrimp, or any other type of food available. We could also drink beer, coke, and whiskey; play cards; or do whatever else we wanted to do.

On the afternoon of the third day, the platoon sergeant came into the bunker as we were playing cards. "Listen up," he said. "We are looking for volunteers for a mission into the north. It's going to be dangerous. The Reds are building a missile base there that will be able to reach our fire bases. We have to take it out, or we will never be safe on our side of the DMZ."

According to the Geneva Convention, any side in a war is supposed to have only eighteen men in the DMZ (demilitarized zone) at one time, but the sergeant thought there was probably a whole regiment of North Vietnamese soldiers there at the time—meaning maybe six hundred and fifty men. To keep our own numbers down, we were going to take only a couple of guys from each platoon to make up our unit.

"I'll walk point," I volunteered. I felt that probably there would be some men who wouldn't be coming back; but, if I did my part, maybe I could make a difference.

My hooch partner, Frank, said, "If my partner is going, I'm going." (A hooch partner is the person who shares a tent with you. Each soldier is given a poncho with snaps on it. When it is time to sleep for the night, the ponchos are snapped together, creating a tent known as a *hooch*.)

Finally, my friend Shamrock, who was from Dallas, said, "To hell with it, man, if one of our platoon goes, we all go. Besides, it makes more sense to have people together who know how the others work, rather than having strangers work together."

"Good," said the platoon sergeant. "Be ready to move out at 0800, so get some sleep tonight."

We were up early, packing our gear and preparing to leave. At 0730, we went down to the chopper landing pad. By 0750, a chopper came in, and, when it finally settled, the company commander said, "Load up."

"Where are the rest of the choppers?" I asked, feeling a little like a rag hung out to dry.

"You know the Geneva Convention rules: we can only take eighteen men into the DMZ. There are already twenty-two of you," the captain said.

"Do you think the Red Chinese and North Vietnamese are playing by the rules?" I asked, more than a little pissed. "What's going to happen when we get back to the river with two thousand mad, armed North Vietnamese after us?"

"**** the Geneva Convention!" Shamrock angrily cut off the captain.

I said, "Sir, I am un-volunteering."

"You can't do that," the captain argued. "I'll go to the battalion commander."

Our group stood in agreement against him. "Go," we argued back. "What are you going to do, send us to Vietnam?" Frustrated, we sat down on the tarmac.

The battalion commander came and asked, "What's the problem?"

I explained the situation as I saw it. He concurred, and soon there were four more choppers on the pads. I was soon known as "the man who started a mutiny." But in reality, the battalion commander simply saw my side of it. And I'll tell you what: I was really glad we had those other troops to cover our backs when we got back to the river. Interestingly, our captain was relieved of duty and posted in the rear. We were given a new captain who wasn't afraid of anything.

When we finally got most of the way to the North Vietnamese missile base, we off-loaded our unnecessary gear and took out only ammunition: frag grenades, extra machine-gun ammo, and, of course, approximately six hundred rounds of rifle ammo each. The six hundred rounds were in three bandoliers of ten clips each, plus one clip in the rifle. The clips would hold twenty bullets, but we loaded them with only eighteen or nineteen, because if you filled them, they would more than likely jam when you really needed them.

When we arrived at the Viet Cong's complex, we saw that it was built much like our own bunkers were. They were dug into the ground and had half-culverts laid on four or five rows of sandbags, with a few layers over the top of the culvert—almost the same as ours. We walked in unimpeded and found probably six or eight AK-47 assault rifles leaned up in teepee fashion throughout the complex.

Our machine-gunner, Tiny, said, "These guys aren't so tough; they ran away."

But I'm thinking, uh oh. They have gone out and surrounded us. "Listen, Tiny," I said. "If they are not here, where do you suppose they are? Everyone, get in the bunkers and get ready. I think they'll be back momentarily."

For a moment, all we heard was the rice boiling in US helmets hung over fires.

And then the Vietnamese came in a bonsai charge—like we had heard took place in the Korean War. They came in a wall, and we fought for survival. Sure enough, there was a whole regiment of North Vietnamese in the DMZ. We were outnumbered about six-hundred-and-fifty to twenty-two.

You can't believe how heightened your senses become in such situations. Your heart is beating out of your chest like a bass drum at a parade, and your adrenalin level is going through the roof. It is quite demoralizing to hear the sound of six-hundred-and-fifty NVA screaming in Vietnamese all at the same time, leaving no doubt about how surrounded you are. You can smell the fear in the air. Any soldier or police officer can attest to this fact, no matter whether they have fought on the streets of the United States, or in Vietnam, or Iraq. We owe all such people a debt of gratitude for the selfless work they do.

On the first charge, with my hair all standing up on my body, my eyes wet from sweat and my heart pounding, I emptied two clips— almost forty rounds—at the enemy; and I was doing my best to keep my head and keep fear at bay. Whenever the fear won, people would lose their lives, and so this situation was no place for giving in to it.

After the charge, bodies were everywhere. Strangely enough, though, when I looked quickly from one side to another, the bodies on the first side would have disappeared. All I could see was the gentle waving of the grass. When I looked back to the other side, the bodies that had been there would have disappeared, too! It didn't matter *where* I looked; I would see movement out of the corner of my eye, but it would prove to be nothing more than waving grass. Soon there were no bodies left—and that included the one just twenty feet from the bunker. It kept the fear and adrenalin going to know that enemies were within twenty-five feet of us, moving bodies, and we couldn't see them.

Then there was the silence. The silence while waiting for something—anything!—to happen was almost as unnerving as the screams. We would use the short break to make sure everyone was okay and the equipment was straight. Then, as suddenly as it had become silent, the air would fill with screams again and the hoard would be back, charging in from all sides. With the second charge, I went through four clips; and again the bodies piled up, and again they disappeared. It was so spooky to know that the North Vietnamese could do that without being seen, considering how many eyes were watching each direction. They were dragging their wounded to the underground hospitals they had all around the perimeter.

As soon as they had policed up all the bodies from one attack, they would charge again, and again, and again, while the bodies continued to disappear quietly down the tunnels. I would have thought we had killed so many that no one was left to hide the bodies. But we were still taking fire, so we called in air support, since we were running low on ammo.

I don't think anyone who hasn't been in such a situation can imagine the terror we felt from those bonsai charges. With the North Vietnamese screaming at the top of their lungs, it was easy to tell how outnumbered we were, and the screams trapped us in a halo of horrendous sound. Twenty-one other people were also having the same feelings I was, living the same terror. All of us were praying. In situations like this, there are no atheists.

Months before this incident, I had learned to aim for "between the blinkers"—meaning the eyes. We had gone into a small village where two VC ran out of a hut, and our Kit Carson scout (a North Vietnamese who defected to our side) opened up on full automatic and knocked one flat in the elephant grass. After he dropped, we couldn't see him. We waited ten minutes, and then, my adrenalin pumping, I went to the spot and found blood all over the matted grass where the VC had rolled around. There was no sign of the body, so we figured the other guy must have carried it away. In the grass-roofed hut was about fifty pounds of rice, which we destroyed.

I set up a mechanical ambush that consisted of a claymore mine and a trip wire along the side of the house. Before we went to our night-defensive perimeter—or, as we called it, our NDP—we set up two more ambushes to protect our guys who were guarding nearby trails. Then we made supper and took turns standing guard.

At 0230, I was awakened by the sound of a claymore going off. I had just gotten back to sleep when another went off. Then I was awakened again when it was my turn for guard duty at 0500. At 0530, just at dawn, I was startled by the sound of a third claymore going off. That sound woke everyone.

You might think we would have rushed right away to check those ambushes. But we were in no particular hurry, because the North Vietnamese would sometimes trip them on purpose with a wire and set up another ambush between you and the one you knew about. Besides, if someone had gotten hit, he wasn't going anywhere anyway, and living on C-rations we were starving all the time.

So everyone started making breakfast and hit the bushes for latrine duty, and at 0700 the sergeant told me to check the ambushes. At the first one we found an old razorback hog. The second one had been set off by some little foxlike creature. But when we got to the village where I had set the claymore, we saw a pair of legs propped up against the wall, where they were cut off above the guy's knees. He was laying there, DOA, with a rucksack on, going to get the rice.

The only thing I found in the dead man's rucksack was a baggie, full of what looked to me to be little round rabbit pellets. The Kit Carson scout was with us, and I asked him what they were.

He said, "I no talk good English. I show you." He took a safety pin off his shirt and stuck it into one of those little balls, lit the ball with a match, inhaled the smoke, smiled at me, and said, "Number Oooonnnnne" in a long, exaggerated tone. The VC had probably been as scared as we were and had smoked opium to try to relax.

Can you understand how it felt to be a trained healer—someone who was supposed to be helping people live—and have to follow orders and kill people? It was such a great sadness for me. I checked the man's body for any paper he might be carrying. When I opened his shirt, I saw that, before the mine got him, he had already had seven bullet holes in him. He had a rag pushed in each hole and another rag wrapped around all of them.

This VC was the same man whom our Kit Carson scout had shot the day before. But he had still had the strength to come back for rice! This is why I learned to shoot for the blinkers— for sheer survival, in spite of the torture this caused within me. What eased the torture a little was that I always tried to take out the enemy who was aiming at me.

So all the time during the VC attack in the DMZ a couple of months later, I had aimed for the blinkers and survived. When the battle was over, the gunships were clearing a path to the south for our escape, and we were starting to depart in groups of two and three. I was just getting ready to leave when one of the gunships mistook us for NVA and fired a missile at us. We were waving to let the pilot know we were friendlies, and, just as he fired, he figured out that we were on his side. He hauled back on the stick, which sent the missile about forty yards past us, and we got down, so no one was hurt.

The only person who had been hit in the intense firefight was our medic, Doc Yamato. He was Pima Indian, and he was hit in the stomach. The wound wasn't as serious as it could have been, but it was enough to get him a free trip home with a purple heart. For this reason, I was happy for the doc.

As we headed for the river, Harold Brown; Frank, my hooch partner; and I ran together. Harold was six feet tall, thin, and had the long legs of an athlete. We ran close to a mile, and, when we stopped for a second to catch our wind, we heard thump, thump-thump. About fifty yards from us, an eighty-two-millimeter mortar round exploded. Then, about twenty-five yards away, a second one exploded; and the third round landed between Harold's feet. Sticking out of the ground were just the top and the fins that make them fly straight. Harold went ashy as he stared at it. I took off, but Harold was still just standing there looking at it.

"Harold!" I yelled. "Maybe it is a time-delay fuse!"

Harold took off in a cloud of dust, passing me like I was running in reverse. It was the last I saw of him until we got to the river. As our unit ran, the rest of our company on the south side of the river was taking fire; but before we got there, the gunships showed up and cleared a nice path for us to cross the water.

After the battle was over, the army filmed the scene with one of those little glass-domed Loach helicopters that had cameras mounted on it. Twenty-two of us had 129 confirmed kills, though, in reality, we probably killed three to five times as many. But it was hard to tell because, as I have said, within minutes of each bonsai charge the bodies would disappear right before our eyes. We had no way to count them. In the end, we must have killed so many that there was no one left to drag the last bodies into the tunnels, and those bodies must have been the ones the army counted—as I later explained to one of the majors when he asked why there were so few bodies at the scene.

As an afterthought, our platoon received presidential citations from both the United States and Vietnam, but only Doc Yamato received a medal—for getting hit. Not one of us who battled the NVA received anything. The radio telephone operator on the south side of the DMZ got a Silver Star for killing twelve guys or something. Perhaps our own platoon didn't deserve anything because, according to the Geneva Convention, we had exceeded the number of soldiers allowed to be in the DMZ at any one time.

While we were in for stand-down, we got our showers and haircuts and then went to the bar, had a couple drinks, and played cards. I went to bed about 0100, got up about 1000 hours, cleaned up, and then went to the chow hall near headquarters. Standing in line, I thought I recognized a guy from stateside. I walked over, and sure enough, it was my old "armor" (the person in charge of guns) from Fort Jackson.

"Hey, Corporal Harvey, do you remember me?" I asked. His face looked like he had seen a ghost.

"I . . . I . . . I . . . re . . . re . . . remember you," he stammered.

"I remember you, too," I said. "You assigned with us?"

"Ya, ya, I'm assigned to Second Platoon, Charlie Company."

"Great! That's where I am. We have three more days of stand-down, so you'd better enjoy them, as where we are going is not fun. We're called the swing company of the swing battalion, so we're always sent into hot landing zones," I told him.

I went on through the line at the chow hall, and Corporal Harvey disappeared somewhere. After stand-down, I looked for him, and the platoon sergeant said he had transferred to a different company.

Harvey wasn't my superior in 'Nam, but he had been at Fort Jackson in the states, where he had treated me very badly. He was black and thought I was white, so he had made me clean my gun over and over again while letting the black kids hand in dirty weapons. After weeks of this kind of discrimination, I told him I would see him and remember him when he got to 'Nam; then the harassment had stopped.

Now, when Corporal Harvey saw me at the chow hall, he must have thought I would exact some kind of retribution, but he really didn't know who I am. As a healer, I would never consider such a thing. Harvey would have been much better off with our company, as, for the most part, those of us who were left had our act together.

Dayglow

D ay after day when I was in Vietnam we walked in the unbearable heat and humidity. The rucksacks we carried always outweighed us, since we were understaffed because of the casualties we had suffered. Whenever the rear echelon resupplied us with food, ammo, claymore mines, bullets and other essentials, they did so as if we were a whole platoon; but, in reality, we were seldom more than two-thirds strong, and sometimes a lot less. So we had so much stuff packed in our rucks that we would have to help each other up with them. And seldom was it cool enough that our clothes didn't stick to us like a wet skin. Every scratch got infected, we constantly suffered from jungle rot because we were never dry, and the leather in our boots rotted.

Any newbies who joined us weren't used to the heat, just as the rest of us hadn't been at first. So we had to watch them closely, because in that humidity, it was easy to be taken out with heat stroke without ever even seeing an enemy—who was far more used to the conditions than we were. The humidity in the jungle was so high that sometimes it felt like we not only were bathed in water but were breathing it. Carrying so much heavy equipment would have been tough even at home. In those days I weighed 132 soaking wet— which we were 90 percent of the time—and my rucksack outweighed me by 50 or 60 pounds. Add the three bandoliers of ammo, which were not in the ruck but on my shoulders, and my total load was near 200 pounds. Having to carry it in such intense heat just made a bad situation that much worse.

Often the Creator God would talk to me. Sometimes he talked in words, sometimes in pictures. I remember, for instance, meeting Bill, a black kid from New York on whose forehead I saw a mark that looked like a Day-Glo watch face without the numbers. I had seen this mark on other soldiers' foreheads, but this was the first time I realized what it meant. The other times I had thought I was seeing things, but then the mark would be gone, and soon afterward the guy would die. When I saw the mark on Bill, I did everything I could to train him. I took him on as a hooch partner. During our first NDP, I asked Bill to cut tent poles while I cleared a spot for our tent. I noticed a couple of old tent poles sticking up where someone had possibly camped before. When Bill started walking over to them, I said, "Don't touch them! They could be hooked to a five-hundred-pound bomb."

Rather strongly, he replied, "But they're already cut, and they're the right size."

"I don't care. You should never, ever pull anything out of the ground. You never know what it's hooked to."

Bill must not have had a gram who taught him always to take the extra minute to do things the right way. I guess I was nagging him too much, always saying, "Don't do this; don't do that; all this stuff is for your own good." Three weeks after he arrived, he transferred to our sister unit, Bravo Company, of the 196th in the Second Battalion, First Infantry.

On Bill's first night with that company, he pulled a stake out of the ground and took out not only himself but a couple of others as well. It was my understanding that the stake was hooked to a five-hundred-pound bomb. They said there was not even enough left of Bill to bag up.

The poor guy had been scared to death of dying. His tragedy brought home to me what my grandmother had said: "Walking in fear, you make bad choices, and whatever you send out to the universe comes back to you amplified and magnified." I started truly knowing that I was going to make it through all this. The situation also showed me I would always spot a booby trap, and I always did.

While in the army, I often found myself thinking of Gram. I thought of all the time and effort she had put into me. So much of her teachings had become part of my being, as though she knew I would draw from her wisdom like a fish needs water.

I remembered a day in 1959 when Gram was gazing out the window and said, "Come look." As I peered through the glass, I saw a feral cat on the hunt. There was also a flock of little brown birds jeering at the cat.

"Just watch," she said. After a while, those little birds put the run on the cat and drove it past the house, clear across Highway 70.

"What did you see?" asked Gram.

"I saw a cat scared by little birds."

111

She corrected me. "You saw a life's lesson."

"How's that?"

"What size are the birds?"

"Really little," I answered.

"So how is it possible for those tiny birds to chase away a critter that is a hundred times their size?"

"There are a lot of them, and they worked together."

"But why?" she urged.

"So the cat couldn't eat them."

"So think about what you have learned."

"Well, if a lot of little things work together, they can take on a big thing," I answered.

"Yes, it is about working for the common good of all. It is about teamwork. Remember this well; you will need it later in life," Gram advised.

Remembering this teaching in Vietnam, when I was surrounded by an entire regiment of NVA (the cat) and the eighteen guys in our platoon (the little birds), I realized that it was finally "later in life." Thank you, Gram.

Tam Kỳ: Hello, Post-traumatic Stress Disorder (PTSD)

In mid-May, 1971, we were sent to Tam Kỳ (Tam Key), the main US military base in what was then the Quảng Tin province on the south central coast of Vietnam. We were an air-mobile infantry, so in one week we could work in several areas of operation. From Tam Kỳ we were flown north and then west and finally dropped in Laos (although, at the time, we weren't supposed to say where we were). We were sent out with three days of rations; then we would be resupplied. But while we were in Laos the monsoon started. Normally during a monsoon the rain starts around four in the afternoon and lasts until five in the morning, so you have some dry periods. But this monsoon was different. Oh, it would rain all night, as usual, and then we would have a couple hours of dryness. But then it would rain again; so every time the rear echelon headed toward us with new supplies, they would have to turn back. Soon we were out of food. Some of the guys were worried, even though where we were was a land of abundance—full of jungle fowl, wild pigs, spotted deer, wild bananas, bamboo shoots, fish, and freshwater shrimp. If you grow up in a city where everything comes from a store, you are not aware of nature's bounty all around you.

When we had been without food for three days, I told the sergeant that we needed to go on a hunt; we couldn't live on nothing. He said to take a patrol but be careful. A few of us went out and came back with a little pig and two jungle fowl. I asked a couple guys to help clean and butcher the animals, but they were from the city and had not a clue. The jungle fowl looked like anorexic chickens on diets, and they didn't make much meat, but it was something. That tough chicken was some of the best-tasting stuff I ever had.

The monsoon still wasn't letting up, and there was no rear echelon in sight. The captain talked to battalion, and they decided that we should walk in. By plane, we were only four or so hours from Tam Kỳ, but walking through the jungle would take us two weeks to get back. So we were going to walk to the more northern base of Da Nang, the nearest base to where we were and our actual rear area. The guys, though, called the walk the "Tam Kỳ Death March"

113

because Tam Kỳ had been the first place we were dropped before we went to Laos.

One reason I liked being in the air-mobile infantry was that we could work an area for a week or two and then—usually, unless a monsoon stopped it—the rear echelon would pick us up and move us, and the VC would have no idea where we had gone. We were always surprising them, moving in and out like ghosts, and they were seldom sure where we were.

But now that we were grounded, the VC had plenty of time to find us. On our extended hike of several days, they were constantly harassing us, going ahead of us and planting booby traps. And when we made our night-defensive parameter, they would get on three sides of us and wait until ten o'clock at night or so, after we had settled down, and then open up with automatic-weapons fire. I don't think they were really trying to kill us; they just wanted to keep us from getting sleep, and they were quite effective!

The constant harassment kept our adrenal glands firing. And, as I have said, when you are eighteen and growing, firing adrenals also grow, just like any muscle gets bigger the more you use it. In a situation where you can fly out (air mobile), the harassment stops as soon as you leave the area. But when you are grounded and have to walk all the way from Laos to Da Nang, the harassment is unending. Pretty soon, your nerves are shot.

If you have ever been startled, you know the feeling: the heart-pounding, the instant sweating, the faster breath. This has happened to everyone at one time or another and is just the mildest example. Imagine this situation magnified a thousand times and you will have a slight idea what PTSD is like.

At its onset, PTSD is as bad as it gets. It damn seldom gets worse, although we rarely recover from it altogether. I have worked as hard as anyone I know to get over it, and, even after all these years, not all the effects are gone. I still have occasional nightmares, night sweats, sleepwalking, and screaming fits in my sleep. But the more I work on it, the more the severity lessens.

Even while other symptoms of PTSD diminish, though, the amount of adrenalin your body produces can increase in response to stress. And the more the adrenalin level increases, the harder it is to figure out what to do with all that energy, unless you're in active combat. Under stress, normal adrenal glands will produce a mere microscopic drop of adrenalin, and that is enough to supercharge a nontraumatized person into action. But if you suffer from PTSD, you may produce a quarter-teaspoon of adrenalin—and, as a combat vet, even a *full* teaspoon—or at least that's what it feels like.

After I was discharged from the military, I underwent twelve years of therapy and found that it provided some useful tools if you actually use them—but there was so much to remember! I found that the old ways are still the best, as I describe them in this book. It was my gram's old Oneida Fire Ceremony that was my lifesaver; I am here because of it—plain and simple.

The Soldier Evolves into a Healer

I arrived home from Vietnam on a Saturday, October 16, 1971. My folks welcomed me with a party and dance. It was there that I met my first wife, Anne. After we danced, I told her I was going to marry her. And so it was, for twenty-five years.

Soon we had a baby boy. My son, Shayne, who was born in 1973, suffered from colic. At the time, I worked on a crew that was building Highway 63, pulling two ten-hour shifts. The poor little guy would cry and cry. One night, when I was very stressed due to lack of sleep, I picked up my son and placed my hand on his stomach.

I said, "Creator, please help me stop Shayne's pain." He stopped crying and never had colic again. Today, it still works. In fact, this year alone I treated six or seven colicky babies with the same results.

A few weeks after I healed Shayne of colic, my wife had a terrible headache and said she couldn't stand the pain. When I put my hands on her head the headache went away, but I developed a slight headache myself. It didn't last long, however, after I thanked the Creator for removing my wife's pain.

On another occasion, one of my coworkers on the building crew hurt his arm. I asked him if I could try to take the pain away, and he said yes. I prayed to the Creator, and the pain went away. However, I then felt pain in my own arm. And again, after I thanked the Creator, the pain disappeared. It didn't take long for me to put two and two together. Among my grandmother's many lessons about healing, I learned that the key to it all was having gratitude.

It wasn't long before the word got out about the crazy 'Nam vet who might be able to do some healing. I began as a closet healer because I did not want a reputation for being crazy. It would be fifteen or twenty years before I committed to healing full time. Other factors also held me back, one being simply the self-doubt that every human has, especially when starting out in a new profession or any life-changing situation.

Most new parents worry whether they are up to the job of raising a child. I wondered if I was up to doing healing work and if I could learn it as well as Gram had. I knew that living up to clients' expectations would be quite a responsibility.

And there were the "what-if" questions to keep at bay. To such doubts Gram had always said, "There is no 'what if'; there is only 'do or do not.' Why do you question the Creator when he made everything, including us? How easy it is for him to do a little repair work, yes?"

"Yes," I would agree. Think, for example, of a mechanic fixing a flat tire. The car is already made, so it is nothing to put a new tire on. It is the same with healing, if you can get out of the way and know with conviction that the Creator can do it.

But for a long time, I still felt ambivalent about healing work, one reason being a question posed by a childhood friend of mine, Jim. Once when I was doing a healing, he asked, "How can you be a healer when you killed people in Vietnam? I saw the newspaper article about how you made soldier of the month by having the most confirmed kills for the Second Battalion, First Infantry; there were a lot of men in that battalion, weren't there?"

"About seven thousand," I said. Jim was a neighbor and one of my best friends growing up. He went to college and later furthered his education and became a minister while I went to 'Nam.

"To tell you the truth, Jim," I said, "I don't have an answer for you yet." It took me five years to finally get an answer for him—and for myself. Long after the experience of fighting, killing, and being a constant target, I concluded that the Creator sent me to Vietnam to gain an intimate knowledge of death. If I had not overcome my fear of death, I could not be the healer I was meant to be. I had to confront the reality of death so that I could work on anyone, no matter what the circumstance.

After I got home, I met several healers with whom I became fast friends. One of them was a woman named Gail. She had an office in Minnetonka, Minnesota. I would visit her once a month or so, and we would have dinner together. She was a very good healer;

her sessions cost ninety dollars for twenty minutes. She was booked three months in advance. One day I arrived at her shop at about a quarter after four and was sitting in the waiting room, waiting for her to be finished at four thirty. An old man came in, unshaven and somewhat dirty, wearing raggedy clothes. In a breathless voice he asked if I was the healer, to which I replied, "I am a healer, but not the one you are looking for; Gail will be out in a minute."

Exactly at four thirty, Gail came out with her female client and set up another appointment with her.

"Hey, how's it going, Russell?"

"It was a nice trip down, and this guy is here to see you."

"What can I do for you?" she asked the old guy.

"I just got back from a test at University Hospital," the man said, again breathlessly. "They say my lungs are full of cancer and there is nothing they can do for me. I wondered if you could help me."

"I'm sorry, but I don't think I am the healer for you. I don't think I can help you."

The old guy frowned with a tear in his eye and then headed for the door.

"Wait!" I said to him. Turning to Gail, I asked, "Can I give him my card?"

"Sure. I can't help him," she said. So I handed the man my card, and he looked at it.

"Spooner; that's way up in Wisconsin, is it not?"

"Yes, it is, but what other choice do you have?"

"You can help me?"

"Won't know until I try," I said.

The man left, still holding my card. Gail and I went to dinner, and as we ate we talked.

"Why wouldn't you help that man?" I asked.

"Listen, I have a very large clientele here, and I can't have clients dying on me. It wouldn't be good for business, and I am very comfortable right now. This is a small town, and word would spread like wildfire."

"Gail, what is the real reason? I am sure it's not that."

"Well, I am just a bit afraid of people who are dying."

"But we are headed for death the moment we are born."

"Well, it scares the heck out of me."

After dinner I headed home and wondered about what I had heard that night. Then it was like the Creator slapped me up 'long side the head. That's when I realized that he had sent me to Vietnam to get comfortable with death. I had given the old man my card because we had nothing to lose by doing the healing. The next week, the old guy—whose name was Nick—showed up, and three weeks later his cancer was gone. He was a most happy gentleman.

During this time, the Creator gave me several signs that he wanted me to do more healing, signs such as more and more people showing up to be healed without my using one bit of advertising. However, I was too busy then with work and raising a family. These factors, along with my occasional falling spells caused by Agent Orange, made it nearly impossible to take on more.

Eventually, I became a blatant workaholic. The steady flow of nightmares I was having about 'Nam interfered with my sleep. I figured that if I couldn't sleep, I might as well work. I used to put in eight hours at my union job, go home to eat, and then work on my own job for six to eight more hours as a masonry contractor. This way, during the week, I could get the basements of new houses ready to lay up on the weekends. I would start on a concrete-block basement on Saturday morning and be finished by Sunday afternoon.

Having a schedule like that allowed me to amass a small fortune over the years. It wasn't until much later that I finally took my path to full-time healing.

Three Little Bumps: Ancient Lands by Way of Texas

The year was 1975, and my wife, Anne, and I were driving across central Texas on our way to Sacramento to visit her relatives. Normally, the driving route from Wisconsin to California would not include Texas, but I didn't want to drive through the snowy mountains in January, so we took I-35 and drove south through central Texas.

As I was driving, I started feeling uneasy. On the horizon I could see three little bumps. The closer I drove toward the bumps, the more uneasy I became. I had been used to this feeling since coming home from Vietnam three years earlier. I guess walking point for seven or eight months in the 'Nam jungle would be enough to make anyone a little uneasy. I wasn't exactly sure why the uneasiness came on, but I thought it might have something to do with the little bumps up ahead. I would soon find out.

Finally I said to Anne, "Do you think you can drive?"

"Why?" she asked.

"I don't know."

She suggested, "Let's stop for the night."

We soon found a roadside motel, and, since it was early, we had no trouble getting a room. Not long after, I fell asleep. That night I had the same dream I'd had when I was three-and-a-half years old, shortly after my grandfather's death. I hadn't understood much of the dream then, but now it made more sense.

In the dream, the year was 1519. My father, the Aztec King God Motecahzoma (better known now as Montezuma), was in Tenochtitlan, the Nahuatl name of our city of 4.5 million people, including the surrounding allied city-states of Tlacopan and Texcoco. At that moment in time, it was the biggest city in the world; later, it would be known as Mexico City.

The Spanish conquistador Cortez had captured my father and threatened to kill him if we didn't pay three chests of gold in tribute to the Catholic Church. So I found Jonee, who was the head of the palace guards in charge of protecting Motecahzoma and the royal family. Jonee had been my teacher and mentor over the years and had become my very dear friend. Together with a Spanish guard, we went to our city center.

We told the forty or fifty city criers to announce that there was a job for eight men—carrying heavy chests of gold. It would be hard, treacherous work, and, when they were finished, their throats would be cut. In the dream, I had no more feeling about telling the peons this than I would have had killing a fly. You have to understand that this was simply our Aztec way at the time. No emotion was involved. Such events were just a fact of life.

But when the Spanish guard heard my announcement, he was mad as hell and hit me with the flat of his sword, leaving welts on my back.

I said, "Are you out of your head?"

"How are you going to find men to haul gold to the missions when you tell them they are going to be killed? We will kill your

father, and it will be your fault. You should have lied to those men!"
he yelled, hitting me again.

"Why waste time worrying about what isn't, instead of thinking
about what is?" I challenged. We Aztecs didn't know what *lying*
meant, because we had no need for it. There was the truth, and that
was all there was. We always spoke truth; we didn't know there was
any other way.

But the Spanish surely knew how to lie. Yet they thought they
were better than we were, even though they didn't follow their own
teachings. They professed the Christian faith, yet in their missionary
zeal it was okay to rape our women and daughters to save the heathens
and bring them to Christ. And they were as uncouth a people as I
had ever seen. We thought the Spanish were filthy pigs. They never
bathed, and they stank in their armor. It was fleece-lined, keeping
their sweat in there, causing the odor to become very rank in the
ninety- and one hundred-degree days. We figured out that, if we put
our hands together, bowed down, and greeted them in Aztec with,
"Hello, swine," or some such thing, they would get big smiles on
their faces and think we were honoring them. It was an inside joke
for years, until they learned some of our language.

Also, we thought it quite funny that the conquistadors burned
us at the stake because they thought we were heathens and didn't
believe in the Creator when, in fact, our heaven had three more
layers than theirs. Our heaven had four layers: The first was the
peons' layer. If you were a good peon, you would make it to that
layer; if not, you ended up nowhere. The second layer was for the
commoners. If you were a good commoner, you would get to it; if
not, you would end up in the peons' layer. The third layer was for
noblemen—good ones would go to it, bad ones could end up in the
commoners' layer or lower. Finally, the highest layer of heaven was
for royalty and royal family members like my brothers, my sisters,

and me. There was one exception: If anyone from another caste died defending our King God, he would earn an instant trip to our royal layer of heaven.

"If you don't find anyone to carry the gold, we will kill your father," repeated the Spanish soldier.

I replied, "Let's wait until morning. There will be more than enough volunteers to carry your gold to the mission church up north."

The next morning, much to the Spaniard's surprise, probably eight thousand peons vied for the eight jobs. We chose eight men and gave them the rest of the day to say goodbye to their friends and family. I did the same.

Asking a favor of my best friend, Jonee, I said, "I feel I am not coming back from this trip. Will you take care of my wife and children after I am gone? I fear the Spaniards cannot be trusted. They are not gods, like my father thinks. They are beasts. As soon as you can, head far into the back country." Jonee agreed.

That night, I told my wife that I wouldn't be coming back. I told her that those animals, the Spaniards, were here to stay. Furthermore, if anything happened to my father, she was to take the children and go with Jonee, running far away, or the Spaniards would rape and kill them. The Spaniards were typically brutal to our people, and I didn't want them near my wife or ten-year-old daughter.

The next morning, eight Spanish soldiers, the eight volunteers, and I headed out with the chests of gold. Each of the three chests was carried by two volunteers; every hour I would have the two extra men relieve two of the gold carriers. We took breaks every couple of hours. In this way, we walked north for days. The days turned into weeks and then months. Eventually, we were at the fringes of our land, which later would be called Texas.

As we walked along near the north end of our empire, I saw three buttes that were all the same height.

"Those buttes are the Three Sisters," said one of the gold bearers.

The Spanish soldiers hunted for deer or desert sheep. Since carrying the gold was hard, heavy work, they fed us well. They needed to ensure that our energy would not become depleted so that the gold would reach their church as planned.

Some months into the journey, while entering some small mountains, one of the Spanish soldiers took a horseshoe nail and a hammer and etched a Spanish cross into the rock. The date appeared to be 1514, but it should have been 1519. Although I have never looked for it, I am sure that this mark is still in the rock today, in the twenty-first century. I would bet that others have seen it, too, and I have a feeling that someone has even photographed it.

About two weeks after the Spaniard's etching, we came to a hillside with a typical adobe Spanish mission, built by native slaves. It had a walkout basement. On the left side of the walkout was a set of steps carved into the rock, going down under the basement floor. The underground room was just big enough to hold the three chests of gold, with three peons standing at the end and five peons standing on the side, and to give me room to do the deed for which I was brought. I told the men to make their peace with the Creator and picked up my lance, which had a huge gold knife on the end. It was shaped somewhat like the C-cleft on sheet music and was very sharp on both edges.

I walked up to the first man and asked if he was ready, and he said yes. I said, "I will try to make this as painless as possible."

He said, "It matters not; the pain won't last long."

I then cut his throat. He never made a sound or attempted to move, nor did the second, third, fourth, or fifth. One of the Spaniards remarked that we were animals because we just stood there and let our throats be cut without attempting to escape. The men would stand for almost a minute with blood running down their chests before they fell down.

I asked the sixth man if he was ready. He said yes. And so it went for the last two. As I watched the last man collapse, I felt a pain in my back and watched the sword emerge from my chest. I could feel my life's blood flowing from me. When the Spaniard pulled the sword out, I spun around and collapsed to my knees.

My wife appeared to me. She was smiling at me and I at her. I told her that I wasn't returning, but that she would be fine as long she took the girl and my son, Takaheychatl, and went with Jonee. (In the Aztec way girls were of no importance; what was important was the male hereditary line of the king. So it was doubtful that I ever knew my daughter's name. She was simply "the girl.")

"You will live in the back country," I said to my wife. "I love you."

She said, "I will miss you, my husband, but I will see that your lineage lives on."

The Spanish man had a look of terror on his face. As I spun around, he stepped back. He obviously could not see my wife and must have thought I was talking to him. As I died, I found it satisfying to know that this incident would haunt him for the rest of his life, because the Spanish considered it very bad luck to be cursed by someone they killed. Although I wasn't cursing him, he would go to his grave blaming me for every bit of bad luck he would ever have from then on.

When I woke up in the morning from this long dream in our Texas motel room, I was suddenly back in current time: 1975. As we were leaving the motel, I asked Anne to drive.

At the time of this trip, I was just twenty-four years old. Yet my unsettling feeling persisted; I found myself unable to shake my sense of uneasiness about those three bumps still visible on the horizon. After four or five hours, we finally reached them: they were buttes.

I said to Anne, "I've been here before."

"How can that be? You've never been to Texas."

I told her that I had walked by this place in a different life.

"You okay?" she asked, looking at me quizzically.

"Yes," I replied.

But it wasn't until after we passed the buttes that I felt relief. They were the Three Sisters—the same three buttes that I had walked past 457 years ago when I had helped transport the three chests of Aztec gold to save the life of my father, Motecahzoma.

The Creator Heals through My Hands

One morning in 1975, while I was laying masonry fieldstone, an old man came walking down the dirt road. Who would have known that I would later do a healing on him that would be pivotal in my understanding of what a healer could do? He walked up the driveway, and as we talked, he found out that I did healing. He told me that his name was Dan and that he had cancer. He said he was hoping just to live out his last days as comfortably as he could. Eventually, he asked, "Can you do anything with cancer?"

"I don't know," I replied. "I have never tried, but I know God can do anything."

I invited Dan into my house and laid him on the couch. I smudged him with sage and asked my family to stay in the kitchen while I did the healing.

While working on Dan, I first started to have an inkling of what was really happening when I did a healing. It was one of the first times I actually listened to the voice in my head that was so often present and would tell me certain things about people. During this healing, I suddenly realized that the voice was the Creator's and that he was communicating with me.

As I moved my hands over Dan's body and sent him love in the form of energy, the voice told me that there were lumps in his lungs. I went over him with the aquamarine light, as Gram had taught me, in order to release whatever negative energy might be there. Then, also as Gram had instructed, I used purple light to send the Creator's love, which is what actually does the healing. The Creator showed me, in my mind's eye, an image of two spiral-shaped strips. I later understood that this was DNA. The strips were slowly spinning, and my eyes naturally followed their spinning ladders down. However, I could not tell one strip from the other. Later, I concluded that when the Creator fixes cancer, he does it by getting rid of defective DNA and replacing it with good.

Finally, I sealed Dan in a cocoon of royal blue light. When the Creator told me that he would be just fine, I felt great relief. This was because it was one of the first times I had worked on someone with a life-threatening illness.

Dan said that I sure seemed confident that the cancer would be gone. I replied, "If the Creator says it is so, then it is for real." He laughed joyfully, as the doctors had told him that he was terminal.

"Hey, the pain has subsided!" he added excitedly.

"I'm glad," I said. "Keep in touch, okay?"

I didn't hear anything from him for six months; then I finally got a call. "Hi, this is Dan, the guy who used to have cancer. I'm calling to say thanks."

"You're welcome, but remember, I am only a man, just like you. I'm merely the instrument," I said. "It is the Creator God who does the healing."

"What do I owe you?" he asked.

"Nothing."

"Well, if I see you uptown, how 'bout I buy you a beer?" Dan asked.

"Good," I replied. I never collected that beer, but it was okay. I learned a valuable lesson about energy exchange. Serving as the medium for Dan's healing by the Creator gave me the first opportunity to understand that doctors do not have all the answers. Previously when I did a healing, I acted according to the words of my grandmother, but without complete faith in the process. I still held onto my mother's beliefs that doctors were gods. This conflict between my grandmother's teachings and my mother's Western belief system took years to unravel. Eventually, I came to realize that doctors are no more gods than I am. We are all children of the Creator—no more, no less.

My Hand Feels an Ice Pick

In about the year 1976, I was doing a few healings every week. The people who were hearing about me then weren't as receptive as the people who would hear of my work twenty years later. In those days, many people, including some family members, thought I had "fallen off my rocker." Nevertheless, I *was* still getting some work, as those I treated told others about me and word slowly spread.

One day, Rob, an elderly gentleman who was a pulp-cutter, stopped by, complaining of losing his ambition and not being able to work as hard as he had when he was younger. As I smudged him up and started working on him, I was thinking that he felt very tired. But then again, what would you expect of an old man who must have been in his early- to middle-forties? (I was all of twenty-five at the time.)

As I was going over Rob's body, I felt something similar to what I had felt in a seventy-nine-year-old man three years earlier. That man had had cancer. But what I felt now wasn't *exactly* the same, and I wasn't sure, so I prayed to the Creator for help: "O Creator of all things, please never let me ever miss identifying cancer." I asked four times, as that is our sacred number. "I implore you so that I may help your children to survive and become more like you."

As I went over Rob's body, when I got to his lungs, even though I couldn't see anything it felt like a red-hot, eight-inch-long ice pick was going through my hand. I yelled and then explained why. When Rob asked what the feeling of a hot ice pick through the hand might mean, I said I wasn't sure, but as soon as I figured it out I would let him know. We arranged that he would come back in two weeks. That gave me time to figure it out. (So, young healers out there, be careful what you ask for, as you may very well get it, and sometimes we know not what that is: I asked the Creator for the ability to detect cancer and got an ice pick in my hand!)

When Rob came back, I did another healing on him and got the ice pick again. "Do you smoke?" I asked.

"Yes, I do. Been smoking for about twenty-five years."

"Do you roll your own or smoke tailor-made cigarettes?"

"I used to roll my own, but in the last ten years the pulp prices have been up, so I've been buying ready-made smokes."

"You know, they are not good for you. We like to blame the tobacco, but, in reality, it's the chemicals the cigarette companies add to make it addictive that are the real culprits," I said. "Anyway, I'm sure it's not good for the lungs."

"I have only been smoking the ready-mades for ten years or so, so how bad can it be?"

"I don't like saying this, but I think you need to have a doctor check your lungs. I feel something, and I want you to get a doctor's opinion. In the meantime, I am going to do some healing on your lungs to see if it will help your tiredness."

"Okay, I'll set up an appointment; but it costs thirty-five dollars, ya know."

"Yes, but it can't hurt to get a different view about what I think I feel, okay?"

"Ya, fer sure," said Rob.

Two weeks went by before he came back. He waited until he had the results of his test.

"What did the doctor find, Rob?"

"I have a spot of cancer on my left lung. It is small, and the doctor said it was a good thing I had him check it, because it seems it is just beginning."

"Good. Lie down, and we will smudge you and get started." I ran my hand over his chest. "Hey! What I was feeling last time seems better now!"

"You knew, didn't you?"

"I wasn't sure, but I thought you might have a spot on your lung there," I said.

"That's why you worked on it last time I was here, right?"

"Yes, and that is why I had you go to the doctor."

"I, for one, am glad you did. They think it will be easy to take care of now, whereas it might not have been if they hadn't found it until a year from now."

"What are their plans?"

"They are talking about surgery, but nothing is decided yet. Do you think I should have the surgery?" Rob asked.

"I can't tell you that. You will have to make up your own mind. I have no fear of working with doctors, but I don't know that they would want to work with me."

Rob said he had another checkup with the doctor the next week and then he would let me know how things stood. It was another two weeks before he showed up again, and when he did he was smiling.

"Hey, you look happy." I greeted him.

"I am. They checked the lump, and it is a centimeter smaller, or maybe it was a *milli*meter smaller. Anyway, the doc says it seems to be shrinking, so he wants to wait a couple more weeks before he makes up his mind."

"That's great! They say that no news is good news—but not always!" I could actually feel that the energy coming off the tumor was lessening, getting weaker with each healing.

"What do you think?" asked Rob.

"It feels to me like it will be gone in a few weeks, but remember, that is only a guess," I said, smiling. "Let's see what the doctor says after your next checkup."

"I have faith in you and your healing."

"Remember what I told you? You should be having faith in the Creator, as he and you are the only ones who are able to save you. I just send the energy where the Creator wants me to."

"Ya, I remember. But *you* are the one I can see," Rob said, laughing.

"Rob, the Creator is with you always. Remember when that tree fell on you? If the Creator hadn't been there, it would have hit your head, and we wouldn't be worrying about healing, now, would we?"

"I guess not. How did you know about that tree falling on me? I never told anyone that."

"Oh, it's a healing thing; that time is still in your heart box—it's a good number of layers down, but there's still enough of it for me to see. By the way, how did the fire ceremony go?"

"It was good; I have a fire ring out by my bus in the town of Chicog, so I did the ceremony there. I had to pick up a pouch of tobacco, and they keep raising the prices. It will be a dollar a bag before you know it."

"There is no doubt about that."

We agreed to meet again after Rob's next doctor appointment. But I never had to see him again, as a couple weeks later he called, happy as all get-out because the lump had disappeared. It had only taken four or five months to heal him, but I still wasn't quite sure what it was I was doing. (And of course I myself wasn't doing it; it was the Creator all the time.)

My next client after Rob was a sixty-year-old man, Gene, who was suffering from cancer of the colon. I was going over his body and praying, and when I got to his lower left colon, I felt the ice pick through my hand again, so I asked him what was going on at that spot.

"I've just been diagnosed with colon cancer, and it is bad. They don't think they can get it out because of the way the roots of the damn thing are growing into my other organs. But you can get it out, right?"

"You are only my second or third client with cancer. I don't want to give you false hope, but the Creator took care of it the other times."

"You worked on old Dan, didn't you?"

"How do you know him, if I may be so curious?" I asked.

"He told me about his cancer, and he sent me here," said Gene, with hope in his eyes.

"Yes, I worked on Dan, and his cancer went away. But you know, I'm not in charge of the healing. Only the Creator has the power to heal."

"Well, Dan is considerably older than me, and if he can beat it, so can I."

"Good attitude!" I said. "One of the reasons Dan's cancer went away is that he did the fire ceremony. I did give him some herbs, but the fire ceremony was the key." I then explained the fire ceremony to Gene and sent him on his way. He came back in a couple weeks reporting that he had done the ceremony and that, at his most recent check-up, the doctor had said the cancer was nearly gone. Two weeks later, it was completely gone.

There have been thousands and thousands of healings since then, and am I still getting the ice pick? When I was forty-four, I prayed to the Creator to take the ice pick away, since by then I knew that he would never miss a cancer, and you know what? I *still* get the ice pick! But over the years I have gotten used to it, so that now it causes hardly more than a discomfort. I think that if I didn't feel it any more, I would probably miss it (as sick as that may sound).

The Creator Teaches Me More about Healing

In 1977, while having a Coke in a bar where I stopped on the way home from laying rock, I ran into a man who knew I was a healer. He had a terrible backache and asked if I could help.

"I don't know," I told him. A voice in my head said to me, as I saw a white light, "Tell him he has a bulging disk." The voice repeated, "Tell him." And so I did tell him, adding that I could help his pain but that he should get an exam and an X-ray.

During the healing, as I held my hands over him, I felt something different in his lower back.

"What is this I'm feeling here?"

"Where?" he asked.

I touched the place and he said, "That's exactly it, the painful spot! I hurt my back working for the railroad."

This is the type of sensory information that I would store away in one of my mental post office boxes. That way, the next time I felt a similar energy from a new person, I had a basis for comparison. Eventually, asking what I was feeling became unnecessary.

A few weeks later, I saw the man in town and asked how he was doing.

"Good," he said. "I was pain-free for four to five days, and then the pain came back."

"Did you do your breathing into the earth and a fire ceremony?" I asked.

"No, but I did as you said and got a test. You saw it right; it is a herniated disk."

This was a perfect example of receiving knowledge through a voice that spoke to me—the voice of the Creator. Eventually I received messages in pictures. I finally understood what my grandmother had said to me so many years before about the Creator speaking to us. I am sure that each of my apprentices will go through the same stages I did of acquiring the skills of a healer. They seem to be standard phases we go through, although new healers may not recognize them at the time. But my gram, her mother, her gram, and I all went through them; I didn't think I was visually attuned enough to receive messages in pictures, but they eventually came.

By 1979 or '80, I was doing a few healings a weekend, and word was starting to spread. One day a man named Bob stopped to see me, saying, "I talked to old Dan, and he told me about you."

"What can I do for you?" I asked.

"Not sure. I have pain in my arm bone, and I would like you to check it, if you would."

"Come in and lie down so I can smudge you off."

"What is that? It smells good."

"It is our purifying smoke that I use before I pray to the Creator."

"It won't hurt me, will it?" Bob looked nervous.

"For heaven's sake, no," I laughed.

"Well, okay then, carry on."

I was praying and going over his body, and, whenever I got to his right arm, the energy felt wrong. I could feel the pain there, but there was something else, too, something unknown to me. The Creator didn't tell me what it was, so I told Bob he should go to the doctor and then come back, because I wasn't sure of what I was feeling.

Bob did go to the doctor and had some tests. A week later, he came back with the results.

"The doc says it is cancer. Can you help me, like you did old Dan?"

"I don't want to give you false hope. All I can say is that I'll do my very best. Let's try."

So I laid him down again; but this time when I went over his arm, I shook my hand, as I felt intense heat.

"What's the matter?" Bob asked.

"I just want to make sure that I don't pick up anything that isn't yours."

"Are you getting a bad sign?"

"I don't know what to make of it. Hopefully it is a sign that the Creator is working on you."

I explained about the fire ceremony and breathing into the earth to release negativity, not really knowing at that time how important it was. Every time I went over Bob's arm, I felt that heat again and had to shake my hand vigorously to get the pain out. It didn't take me long to figure out that heat and cancer are associated.

Bob did his fire ceremonies and breathing, and I had to remind him to ask for what he wanted. But, after about the fourth healing, the heat and pain were gone, and Bob got a clean slate from the doctors a few weeks later.

I always tell my clients to know that this healing will work. Don't just *believe* that it will work, but *know* that it will work. If clients know the healing will work, then they are truly out of the way; and if they are out of the way, the Creator can truly work his magic. As people start understanding this lesson, they find that the healing progresses much faster.

It is always a good feeling to see the Creator's miracles firsthand. It leaves no doubt as to who is doing the healing, and it sure helps keep the ego in check—which I have needed. A few years after I saw Rob, Gene, and Bob, I was getting more and more clients. And the more healings I did, the more miracles I saw. That, of course, gave me a swollen head, and soon I felt like I was doing the healing myself. Soon it was "I did this" and "I did that." For a couple years I was sure that I could do no wrong, no matter what type of healing it was. The more people who came, the more who were healed, and the bigger my head got.

Then I had a client with a simple thing like gout.

"Can you help gout?" asked Marg.

"Of course I can! I can do anything," I said with a big ol' smile. I worked on her, and something was wrong. I couldn't put my finger on it, but it seemed to me the pain from the gout wasn't lessening even after a half hour of healing.

"Is your pain any better?" I asked.

"I don't think so; seems the same to me."

"Let me get you a tea to try."

So we tried this tea and that tea, and nothing I did for the woman seemed to help. After a few more healings with no change, while I was doing my prayers one morning at daylight, I was holding my tobacco up as the sky turned red.

"Creator, why is it that nothing I am doing is helping Marg with the gout?" I was shocked at the answer that came:

"You don't need me. You can do it; you said so yourself."

"You know I didn't really mean that. It was just . . . I guess I was feeling a tiny bit smug about how good the healings have been going. I felt for the first time that I was someone."

"Well, then, go do them! I want to see how far you can go without me."

"No, please; I truly know who does the healing, and it's not me. I know it's you, so won't you help Marg? She need not be punished because of me. Take it out on me if necessary, but don't continue to let someone innocent be hurt by my doings."

"Go heal her," was the reply I got. And since that moment, not one day has gone by without my being clear with people about who can do the healing. It's not me, for sure—it's God. The sooner we know that as healers, the healthier and better off the world will be. We must strive to keep our egos in check, or else get used to the turmoil of life that the ego always seems to bring about and thrive on.

A Sacred Design

Back in 1976, I had an unusual dream in which my spirit guide, whose name I still did not know, came for a visit. I found myself walking with him up the sacred hill to where he had taken me when I was five and lost in the woods. In the dream my guide said, "The time has come to bring the sacred lodge back, which hasn't been used in a few hundred years. The design of the sacred lodge is a whirlwind. No one takes the time to honor it, to build it in the manner that is needed, but the extra time is more than worth it."

We continued walking up the hill. I wanted to ask a question that was formulating in my mind. I could feel it, smell it, and even taste it. I could hear it in my head, but I could not make it come out of my mouth. As hard as I tried, it made no difference. I couldn't ask him his name. I guess the time was not yet right to know it.

We arrived at the top of the hill to see a willow structure standing there. It was made in a manner that resembled two people—each one grabbing his own wrist and one of the other guy's wrists—to make a spiraling, whirlwind design that you might see in a petroglyph.

"This is one of the most sacred designs, but it is a hard model to keep low to the ground like a regular sweat lodge. You would need five or six people to hold it down while you put the cross-rafters over the top. So if you don't have five or six helpers, the lodge will end up higher than a regular one. But not to worry, because the power of this lodge will be stronger than most others," said my spirit guide.

Although in the dream he taught me how to construct this sacred sweat lodge, the reality of it wouldn't come about until 1996. My guide had said that this structure would help rid my fellow veterans and me of the effects of Agent Orange. I found the five or six men needed to hold the initial four lodge poles down, and we constructed the lodge according to my spirit guide's instructions.

Then a medicine man from South Dakota came to try it and said the lodge was much too high; it would never heat up enough to break a sweat, which is what a sweat lodge is all about.

The long and the short of it is that, when we all did a sweat, the medicine man from South Dakota passed out in the third round, and the rest of us finished the sweat ourselves. Eventually the medicine man woke up and we got him cooled off. When he could talk, he said, "Let this be a lesson to you younger guys: don't ever tell the Creator that his sacred places won't work, or he will show you as he just showed me. No matter how long you been a medicine man, you are never too old to learn."

Ever since that experience with the sacred lodge, I have remembered what the South Dakota medicine man said and tried always to stay out of the way when the Creator is doing a healing through me.

During the mid-1990s, I found myself volunteering at the VA hospital in Minneapolis. I was doing healings with elder native men. It was here that I met a Vietnam veteran named Caroline, who was dying of cancer.

"Can you help me?" she asked. "I heard from some of the native men here that you have been helping them with their pain and whatnot."

"Of course," I replied.

"Even though I am black and not red?" she added.

"What matter does that make? We all bleed the same color blood."

She said the VA had given her five days to a week to live and told her she'd better find homes for her six children and make arrangements at the funeral parlor. She smiled and then asked me to do a crossover ceremony to help her die well without having so much pain. I asked her if that was what she really wanted, death being a solution that was really permanent.

"Just think about it," I said as we parted.

Caroline had learned about my work from a Ho-Chunk chief at the VA. I often did the healings on a large hill west of the hospital. The natural setting and the high elevation brought us closer to the Creator. This particular location seemed to help clients focus better, even if they had to make some effort to get up the hill.

The day I worked on Caroline, also going up the hill were the Ho-Chunk chief and a couple other native veterans. The chief was wheelchair bound, and the other Ho-Chunk men were making the effort to push him and his chair to the top. It took considerable work.

As Caroline and I walked up the hill, she asked me if God could take the cancer away. I told her that *I* knew the Creator could take the cancer away but that *she*, herself, had to know it. It required more than just believing. She said that, yes, she knew the Creator could do this. After hearing her response, I said, "Then let's do a healing."

At the top of the hill, Caroline lay down on the earth. As I moved my hands over her, I truly grasped for the first time what the Creator was showing me. Inside my mind, I saw the ladder-like double helixes of her DNA turning. Our DNA is contained in our genes, and every single cell in our bodies has many thousands of genes. We inherit pairs of genes from our parents, one half from our mother and one half from our father. When my eyes followed the double helixes down in Caroline, I could see how one gene in a pair was defective and one was normal. In the normal one, each half of its DNA segment looked like the other; but, in the defective gene, one half of the segment looked normal and the other half looked completely different.

Genes, based on the codes in the DNA, are what tell our cells what to do. Every gene has a "check" function that controls cell division and thus health. When a cell is diseased, during its division a normal gene will tell the good half of the cell to live and the diseased half to die off. But if the gene itself is defective—in this case, coded for cancer—its check function doesn't work; the diseased half of the cell is allowed to divide and divide over and over again, and a couple billion cells later you have the tiniest tumor.

In a healing, when a cell divides, the Creator zaps out the diseased new cell and allows only the healthy new cell to replicate. The cancer lasts only as long as the cells take to divide and become normal.

This is the process that was set into motion that day on the hill when I worked on Caroline. After her healing, I worked on the chief and the other two men. We finished with a pipe ceremony, and I was interested to learn that the Ho-Chunk word for the pipe and the Lakota word for the pipe were the same: *Canupa* (Chen new pa).

In about two weeks, Caroline called. "You know, I am feeling better and my lumps are disappearing."

"That's how healing is *supposed* to work," I joked. Then she called again with the results of her test and invited me to dinner. Needless to say, her cancer was gone in a matter of weeks. In fact, the VA called her a month later to find out why she hadn't died. She told them that God and a healer had saved her.

Now, when I think of the whirlwind sweat lodge my spirit guide had taught me about twenty years before I worked on Caroline, I am struck by the similarity of its structure to the twisting-ladder structure of DNA. If DNA were viewed looking into its rungs from the top or bottom instead of from the side, it would be easy to see how the pattern of the lodge's cross-rafters mirrors this most basic and powerful energy in our bodies. The design of the whirlwind lodge was a sacred design, indeed.

My Spirit Guide Leads Me to My Land

Six years out of the army, in 1977, I was still having nightmares about the Vietnam War. I was dreaming and waking up every hour. So I would get up and design things. One morning, it was about 3:45 a.m. when Anne got up and saw that I had sketched some lines on a piece of paper. I was designing a house. She looked at all the lines and the zigzags with a square in the middle.

"What the heck is that?" she asked.

"That's going to be our new house, when we can build it," I replied.

With a puzzled look, she said, "You better get some sleep. You have to get ready for work in a little over an hour."

Fourteen years later, in 1991, I met with my spirit guide once again. I *still* did not know his name, but by now I was fully aware that he was, indeed, my spirit guide and not just an old Indian guy who had taught me about herbs, rocks, and native beliefs so many years ago. I remembered fondly how he had guided me through the big woods when I was a child, and I remembered with gratitude his teaching me how to build a sweat lodge in the sacred design.

Now, in a vision, he was guiding me to a property on Highway A to show me where I was to build the house. The garden I had designed for it was just the right size to fit around the small burial mound on the property, and my guide instructed me to build the house around both. I thought it was a great property, but it didn't appear to be for sale. Even so, I decided to show it to my wife the next day.

As we arrived at the property, a man was driving away. He had just finished putting up a "For Sale" sign. I felt inspired and took this as an omen. We parked along the road and proceeded to walk out to the spot that my spirit guide had shown me.

As we walked around, my wife said, looking at the burial mound, "I don't like it here. It makes the hair on the back of my neck stand up. We're not going to buy this land. End of story."

But, I just didn't want the opportunity to pass. When we got back out to the road, I took the sign down and put it in the ditch. I took Ann home, drove to town, and paid cash for the property. Gram had always said that if the Creator gives you something, you'd better act on it, or he will think you don't need him and quit sending you gifts.

After I completed all the paperwork for the land, I went back to the property with a couple hundred stakes. My spirit guide had shown me exactly where to put the house. I spent about twelve hours placing the stakes in the ground and adjusting them so that the garden and the house were square with each other. (As I built it, the garden is inside my house in an atrium and the burial mound is mostly under the garden.)

By the time I had finished, I was dog-tired. I went home, ate, and crashed. I had been sleeping about two hours when my spirit guide shook me awake and said, "You have to move the house."

"No," I said. "I put it where you said I should."

I was nearly asleep when he woke me again, repeating, "You have to move the house." Apparently, when I squared it, I pulled the house off site just a bit. After being awakened a few more times, I finally agreed to move the stakes. The next day, I moved them three feet to the southwest. For some reason, the house corners were supposed to sit on the compass points, rather than line up parallel to the road. It took about eight hours to move 150 or so stakes. Needless to say, by the time I got home, there was no time to talk about the new house or play with the kids.

They were chatting amongst themselves as I ate, and they were very excited about having their own rooms. After the ten o'clock news, I went to bed. Again, about midnight, my spirit guide awakened me, saying, "You have to move the house."

"I moved the house today!" I responded.

"It's not right. You have to move it again," he replied.

Being very tired, and after much discussion, I finally agreed, but only because my spirit guide is stubborn—to say the least—doesn't need any sleep, and, as far as I can tell, is always right. So I asked, "Where now?"

My spirit guide pointed south-southeast and said, "Two steps."

The next day, again I moved the stakes—this time about six feet. All the while I was arguing with myself over why I was doing this. "You agreed to it, Stupid," I told myself. It was eight or nine hours later when I had finally finished and went home.

That night, I couldn't sleep. I was tossing and turning, expecting my spirit guide to show up. Finally, about one o'clock in the morning, I fell asleep and dreamed of the house. I walked in the front door of my finished home and instantly saw that my spirit guide was there. A party was going on in the atrium. The joyous, beautiful people there clearly belonged to an earlier age. There was an old, white-haired lady wearing a leather dress with quillwork and a man with long white hair, in a breechcloth and leather leggings, also with quillwork. His apron had a flower design on it. I also saw a couple of native men whose faces were covered in paint. One man's head was shaved from the center to the right. The other fellow had long hair. Both wore aprons beautifully designed with flower motifs. They wore no leggings. A beautiful young girl of about sixteen or seventeen wore a pretty beaded dress, with beads not of glass, but of a much older style, sandcast. Some of the beadwork was done with tiny purple clams the size of a dime. I saw two boys of about five and fourteen years of age and a girl who appeared to be about seven.

In this dream, everyone was happily conversing and joking around. I don't recall ever meeting people so happy and full of funny antics. Although they didn't know me, or I them, they were very receptive to my being there. (That was probably because they were in my house, or maybe I should say I was in theirs.)

Still in the dream, my guide and I went from the atrium to the interior, and I took a good look around. It was just as I imagined it would be. It was different from any house I had ever seen. That was because I had been in a major fit of post-traumatic stress disorder when I designed it. We walked through the living room, the dining

145

room, the kitchen, the garage, the laundry room, the bedrooms, and the family room. We returned to the atrium, where I saw that, while having a great time, one of the young warriors walked into the house. He entered, not through the door, but right through the concrete wall at the east corner.

Of course, I woke up sorry that I had to leave those people. I wrote a note to myself on the nightstand: "Put library in living room, next to patio door at end of hallway, next to our bedroom."

I Finally Learn My Spirit Guide's Name

I started building the new house in 1995. At one point, as I dug out the basement I found a bone that looked too big to be a deer bone. I thought it might be an ancient elk or even buffalo bone.

A year later, Anne, my children, and I moved in. The first night we were there, my son Travis went to bed early and my daughter, Ashley, and I were watching television. At 9 p.m. we heard a blood-curdling scream coming from Travis's room. I ran down the hall toward the sound, Ashley behind me. It being our very first night in the house, I couldn't find any light switches in the dark. I finally located Travis's door and opened it, but before I could turn on the light Ashley ran into me and knocked me in to the pitch-dark room. God, I thought! I'm in here with maybe a murderer and I can't see a thing! Finally I reached around Ashley and got the light on. There was my son, stiff as a board in bed with his eyes as big as saucers.

Ashley poked me in the ribs and said, "Dad, look," pointing to Travis's legs. There was the imprint of someone's rear end in Travis's blankets right across both his legs.

When I asked Travis why he screamed, he said, "Because this old Indian is sitting on me!"

"Is he hurting you?"

"No, I just can't move my legs. There's no weight on them, but I can't move them. Make him move, Dad!"

"Well, Travis, I can't make him move. But he must be a good spirit, because if he wanted to hurt you he could have done it before I got here. What does he look like?"

"He has black, shoulder-length hair and he is *old!*"

"Old like me or older?" I asked.

"Oh, no, not nearly as old as you."

"Has he said anything?"

"Yes, he said his name is Chitaguah."

At my suggestion, Travis politely asked the spirit to move. Now it was Ashley's turn for widened eyes, as the print of the rear end in the blanket promptly disappeared.

"You okay, Travis?" I asked. My son sat up, jerked his legs right up under his chin, and nodded.

The rest of the night was uneventful. But in a funny way, certain events all seemed to fit together—my spirit guide leading me to my land, then finding the bone when I dug the basement, and, finally, learning my guide's name from my son, when I myself had never been able to voice the words to ask what it was: *Chitaguah!* I have since asked elders from several nations what the name means, but it comes from a much older language than anyone can now remember.

Sleep Puts Me Back in 'Nam

Back in the early 1980s, I had decided that I wanted to do something different, since I had been laying rock and doing concrete finishing for close to twenty years. So, for a change, I decided to attend pipe-welding school in Waukesha, Wisconsin, near Milwaukee. It was too far to commute, so I had a room at the YMCA. My roommate, Mike, and I were on the third floor. Our room was simple. It had concrete walls, with a window and two beds.

I was still having nightmares from my service in Vietnam. One night, after falling asleep, I woke up in the early morning with barely enough light to see. I was feeling my way around inside a Vietnamese mud hut, though I wasn't sure how long it had been since the Viet Cong put me there. I found the window and looked out to see a couple Viet Cong guards sleeping on the grass three feet below. I was trying to get out the window when a voice in the dark said, "What are you doing?"

"The guards are sleeping, and if I can open this window, I'm going to crawl out and escape."

"Hey, Russ, you'd better wake up. You're sleepwalking," said Mike.

"Shhhh," I responded. "You'll wake the guards."

"*Wake up!*" Mike yelled, and slowly the inside of the mud hut became painted concrete walls. Mike miraculously changed back into himself and said, "It's a good thing you weren't able to get out that window. It would have been a long drop."

Yes, it would have been. I climbed back into bed, rolled over, and fell back to sleep. Several similar incidents occurred until I finally did my first fire ceremony years later.

I started going to therapy because I wasn't getting any sleep to speak of. My therapist told me that I had to forgive myself for all those people I had killed in Vietnam. On his advice, I forgave myself over and over and over. But still the nightmares came. The dead Vietnamese came—looking at me with those gray faces and those bluish-gray, dead eyes. They would talk to me, their mouths moving, but I was never able to hear them. It scared the hell out of me.

Seeking help from the VA, I went to see Dr. Horowitz, who set me up with the Abbott Northwestern Hospital Sleep Clinic. They studied me for six twenty-four-hour periods. They wired me up and had a camera on me twenty-four hours a day. In the six-day study period, I slept an average of two and three-quarters hours per night, in ten- to twenty-minute segments.

After the first test, the doctor talked to the nurse who had spent the night monitoring me. He asked her, "Sleep apnea?"

"No, I don't think so," she responded. "If you look at his brain scan, he falls asleep in forty to sixty seconds and starts dreaming in less than a minute after that," she said.

"It's not possible to begin dreaming that early in a sleep cycle," Dr. Horowitz noted. "We'll see what happens in the next test."

Two weeks later, I found myself back at the hospital. I was getting my skin sanded so that the electrodes leading to the brain and heart monitors would remain glued on. They wanted to ensure that I wouldn't try to pull them off in my sleep.

This time, there was a different nurse on duty. I lay down at nine o'clock. I was dreaming by 9:03, and, ten minutes later, I awoke from the first nightmare of the night. And so it went, throughout the night.

Again the doctor talked to the nurse. And again the nurse said, "Doc, it looks like the man goes to sleep, starts dreaming, and wakes up from a nightmare. Look at these charts when I set them side by side."

"Yes, but look at the breath charts, which show that, every once in a while, he stops breathing," said the doctor.

"Well, have you asked him about it?" she asked.

"Yes, he said something about when he walked point. If he heard something, he would stop breathing until he figured out what and where it came from."

"Do you suppose he's walking point in his dreams?" she asked.

"I doubt it," answered the doctor. "No one can have this many dreams."

"Were you ever in the Vietnam War, doctor?" she inquired.

"No," he said, "I was in school."

"Well, maybe we should walk a mile in his shoes."

I returned after two more weeks. The test results were the same. This time, the doctor focused on the breathing. "In the next test, in two weeks, we are going to try an apnea machine."

"What will that do?" I asked.

"It will breathe for you."

"My breathing is fine."

"We will know for sure if this helps, after the next test."

So, two weeks later, they hooked me up to the apnea machine. After seven hours of no sleep, the nurse took me off of it. Finally, I was able to grab a little sleep. When the nurse showed the chart to the doctor, she said, "See here? No sleep for the time he had the machine on. It was like torture watching him try to go to sleep."

After one more attempt to get a different result, they finally came to the conclusion that my sleep problem was a side effect of PTSD. All they could do was to help me learn to live with it. When I told the doctor that I was Native American and I was going to try our methods of treatment, he looked at me like I was nuts and said, "Well, do what you have to, because we ourselves can do very little."

In addition to being part German, my father was also Dakota and Ojibwa. This may not have been exactly the best genetic combination in the world, because it made him a tad on the stubborn side, to say the least. I must have picked up a bit of that stubbornness from him, because, when my wife suggested I do the fire ceremony about my sleep problems, I said no. Being young and dumb and stubborn, I told her that my gram had given me the ceremony to share with *other* people—being a healer, I didn't need a fire ceremony myself. (*Ya, right!*) But after all the tests and trials at the VA didn't work, I went home more than a little depressed, and once more my wife said, "Are you sure you don't want to do a fire ceremony?" So I wrote out my first fire ceremony and burned it. I didn't notice a lot after the ceremony but thought, what the heck.

That night, for the first time in years and years of not sleeping, I slept for eight hours straight through, without waking up once. It was like being in heaven after all those thousands of sleepless nights. I have now just finished my hundredth fire ceremony; if I had gotten the idea to do it right away, my life would have been so much easier. It makes me smile when I teach teenagers to do the ceremony; now their lives will so much better than they would have been. Yes, it is this important: all the years of therapy and sleeping pills never helped as much as that one fire ceremony did. Don't be stubborn like I was. Save yourself a lot of grief. Do the fire ceremony and help yourself.

Revisiting PTSD

Veterans and civilians alike suffer from post-traumatic stress. It makes no difference which war you were in, be it on a front line or, like in Vietnam, surrounded by a circle of enemies you can't see. Alternatively, your own front line might be an abusive relationship or an abusive childhood.

Being trapped in a home where sexual, physical, or mental abuse is prevalent and persistent is, in fact, no different from being trapped in a war zone. PTSD can also be brought on by something like a severe car accident or a chronic or acute disease like MS or cancer. Or it might be triggered by the abuses of the medical system itself, which treats you in a way that's not effective and which seems to get its grip on you and never wants to let go. I sometimes think this tenacious hold exists to feed the egos of the people who think they are helping. But they really can't be of much help when, in most instances, they have not been where the sufferers have been or done and seen what the sufferers have. It is easy for a healing professional to read a textbook and say, "That's what PTSD is," but you don't actually know unless you have walked a mile in the moccasins of someone who has it. I am not here to judge, but the fact is, if we are trying to help without truly knowing how, then we are interfering with the healing process.

PTSD is an ongoing creature that is always with us. I know that it is part of me; it can't be left in a garbage can somewhere. If we could do that, I would have done so many moons ago. So what are the alternatives? We can wallow in self-pity and be victims, or we can try to learn to live with it. Or, we can ignore it, but then it will always come back to bite us when we are not looking.

Let's look at ignoring it. You can go through a normal day weepy, angry, or flying into the rages you developed to help you to survive when you were in combat or any other kind of terrifying, abusive situation. After I came home from 'Nam and before I sought help, the smallest things could set me off, anything that I had no control over—and that is just about everything in the world outside a war zone. In a war, at least you have a weapon; you know your enemy and know what to do if you have to. But you can't solve problems that way back in civilian life, although some people try to and end up in jail.

My reaction was, first, rage: immense anger swelling from the bottom of my soul, welling up like a volcano, then exploding at the only people I felt safe enough to vent at. This is one of the reasons that the divorce rate among veterans is typically much higher than the national average.

PTSD frequently also leads to suicide. The *Journal of the American Medical Association* (Feb. 13, 1987, 790–95) indicated that, for every non–Vietnam War veteran committing suicide, there were 1.7 suicides among Vietnam vets during the first five years after discharge. And CNN has said that the number of vets who take their lives every day is now twenty-two, which is almost one per hour. One retired VA psychiatrist reports that the total number of suicides among US veterans is twenty thousand. That is, suicides accompanied by actual suicide notes. The large numbers of gun deaths that occur with no notes are called "accidents." If you recall, I have said that we vets are a reactionary force; for the most part, we don't *act*, we *react*— and sometimes this includes picking up a gun and sticking it in our mouth and pulling the trigger.

Part of the difference between the Vietnam War and previous wars was their degree of constant intensity. In WWII, the men would be on the front lines for days or weeks, but then they would get to pull back to rest and recuperate, usually for as much as two weeks to a month. But in Vietnam, we would get only three days off to play cards or whatever, and then it was right back out to the field. And when you can't get away from the combat zone, even when nothing is happening, the slightest sound can trigger your "fight or flight" response and set your adrenaline going. At least, that is what happens in soldiers, and I am sure it is no different in anyone else who suffers repeated trauma.

Neanderthal skeletons indicate that those early humans were right-handed and thrust their spears with their right arms. Archeologists came to this conclusion because the right arm bones of the skeletons are almost half again as large as the left arm bones. What happened to the Neanderthals' arm bones is no different from what happens to the adrenal glands in war. Most of the people who go to war are so young that their bodies are still growing, including the adrenal glands—and, like any muscle or bone, those glands get stronger with use.

In Vietnam, where the enemy was all around us, the adrenal glands were firing 24/7. And any time the adrenals are firing like that, they naturally grow, with the result that—even back in civilian life—the usual stresses of life cause veterans to produce several times the amount of adrenaline that a nontraumatized citizen would. Yet the Veterans Administration refuses to acknowledge that the amount of time spent in stressful situations has anything to do with veterans' PTSD! Who knows for sure? I know that I have PTSD because I was in the infantry in Vietnam.

I have been told that my own adrenal glands are the size of a quarter dollar, rather than half the size of my little fingernail, like they should be. When I get disturbed just after waking, I don't have the control I might have when I'm fully awake; and so—with a quarter-teaspoon of adrenalin flowing through my system—I sometimes react in ways I wouldn't necessarily do. For example, across the field from my house is a stop sign at an intersection. One morning when I was sleeping, a neighbor who drives an old, late-'40s, four-cylinder truck came up to the stop sign and pushed his clutch in. The truck made a muffled pop-pop-pop sound as he rolled to a stop. That pop sound instantly put me back into a dream about a mortar attack I was in at Khe Sanh. I guess it was due to the ever-vigilant point man I had been.

So I awoke with a start and half a teaspoon of adrenalin in my system before my eyes were even open. My defensive move was to try to get under the bed, but if I had kept a gun in the bedroom I might have been firing it before I was fully awake. It would have been the result of being in 'Nam, where, if we were startled out of sleep, by the time we were actually awake we could already have been firing our weapons at the enemy for several seconds. This is one reason why so many veterans and other sufferers from PTSD end up in prison: again, we don't act, we *react*, and usually with dire consequences. And we are trying to cope with a thousand times more adrenalin surging through our body than the ordinary person has.

If the court system of the United States would take this reality into consideration, it would be more likely to get people with PTSD help rather than to prosecute them. No excuses; even if we have PTSD, we must still try to use our heads in tense situations. But there are a lot of wounded people out there.

The saddest of sadnesses is that PTSD is contagious. If you deal with or live with someone who has it, you can develop symptoms yourself. In the earlier years, I noticed that my kids and spouses began acting just like I did, and I didn't like it. I am sure that if you have PTSD you will recognize the truth in what I am saying.

Over time, I have adjusted somewhat, but one of the things that still bother me—as you might guess from the pop-pop-popping truck—are loud noises. Fourth of July fireworks took me thirty years to get used to, and I still don't like them. In the early years, I would just bunker up during the Fourth or any other holiday that had fireworks. The first time I had the bright idea to go watch the fireworks, I told my wife I thought I could handle it. I did okay until they shot off one of those four-inch mortar rounds. There is nothing pretty about them; all they do is explode. Well, it went off, and I don't know how, but I found myself under my Pontiac GTO. The clearance of a Pontiac GTO is about six inches off the ground, and they had to jack the car up to get me out. After that, I began spending every Fourth of July on Rainy Lake, up in Ontario, Canada, on an island forty miles from anywhere.

Another thing that bothers PTSD sufferers is people who invade their personal space. We can't stand confrontation, because, when we are pushed, we fall back into reaction mode and usually in a big way. We are far too controlling, and, when we realize it, go too far the other way and act as if we don't care at all—but then the tension builds up in our heart boxes until there is an explosion. We don't like to be wrong and will go out on a limb to prove ourselves right. Sometimes, even when we know we are wrong, we will fight it clear into the pit; then, after crawling out on our bellies, we *might* apologize. I am not making excuses for PTSD. It just is what it is.

On the other hand, people with PTSD are likely to go out of their way to avoid conflict in general. For instance, if some expensive product I've ordered online proves to be inferior, I sometimes settle for it rather than confront the system. Believe it or not, if you have PTSD, accepting something wrong seems easier than challenging it, because when we face conflict, we lose control, and the confrontation can escalate in an ever-more-heated spiral. Not that it necessarily *would* escalate, but we fear that it would. And that leads back to my point about pretending not to care: If you don't care, then whatever the wrong thing is just doesn't matter and your adrenalin is less likely to go off. Avoiding conflict is a coping technique that most PTSD sufferers knowingly or unknowingly have.

I don't like large crowds, because there is no possible way to have the remotest semblance of control when you go to places like malls or supercenters. For years I tried shopping at a supercenter at Christmastime; and I would find that sometimes, even with a cart full of things, I would bolt. I finally figured out that, if I shopped at three o'clock in the morning, most people were sleeping, and I would only run into other PTSD sufferers. So if your mate who has PTSD doesn't want to go to shopping, it is not that they don't want to spend time with you; it is just the pretentious, aggressive crowds and the lack of control that every victim of PTSD feels in such situations.

Change seems to be another thing that PTSD doesn't like. Before being in Vietnam, I used to love to travel; afterward, I found myself bunkering up. The same is true of many others. Some build places out of the way, with signs on their properties saying things like "Trespassers will be shot on sight," or "Trespassers will be prosecuted to the fullest extent of the gun," or "I shoot first and don't ask!" These are all signs I have seen in northern Wisconsin, out in the sticks. I have even found concertina wire, and lord knows where that came from. (Concertina—or razor—wire comes in huge coils and is used by the military to form impenetrable obstacles.) I myself, though, am now getting back into traveling again. The healthier I become, the easier it is to take trips to places I have never been before, and I think that most PTSD sufferers would find this to be true.

Other coping defenses we use include overworking, underworking, using intimidation, literally running away from uncomfortable situations, or doing the opposite by attacking. Because I could never sleep due to my nightmares, I became a workaholic, figuring that if I couldn't sleep I might as well be working. We—the people of PTSD—are usually driven to extremes! There is not much middle ground with this disorder. It is usually an all-or-nothing beast. We tend to dwell on things to the point of becoming obsessive.

Being able to hold down a job is another common problem. Often people with PTSD have to find just the right niche to be able to cope. I found mine in construction, especially laying rock. I was my own boss, which is no picnic with PTSD, because I had to deal with all the stress myself of problems like the concrete not arriving on time or the block truck not showing up because of traffic. But at least I got to work alone and no one would bother me.

What are other problems of PTSD sufferers? There are always the dreams. Accident victims may relive the accident over and over in their dreams until they get to the point of not sleeping for fear of them. Abused people may relive their abuse in their dreams and so also have difficulty sleeping. Sleeplessness can lead to painful fibromyalgia, which in itself is a self-perpetuating disease. Lack of sleep prevents the nerves from healing, which causes pain and swelling, which causes more lack of sleep, and around and around it goes. All victims stuck in their own tragedy can be plagued by this kind of vicious cycle. My gram's herbs and a mineral course helped me get over my own fibromyalgia, together with finally getting sleep after doing the fire ceremony she taught me, as I have described.

It is not that you can't learn to live with PTSD, but it is a real beast until you figure it out. Figuring it out and trying to improve is the key. Falling into the victim mode is easy, but it is no life for anyone. And one thing that makes it easy to fall back into the trap of being the victim is the way society labels us as "crazies." I never liked or used labels myself, but they are a societal reality.

I was in the "poor me" mode for a very short while I tried therapy. But while therapy was helpful in giving me some tools, it didn't really help much until I also used my grandmother's fire ceremony, and even this I fought against for years before I did it. Once I used the ceremony, I found the results amazing, and it seriously changed my life. Not that my PTSD is totally gone, but it rears its ugly head less and less the more fire ceremonies I do.

Other than the fire ceremony, I learned one of the best techniques I know for coping with PTSD from studying my friend Billy Bob Thornton's acting. In acting, you can pretend to be mad or aggravated while, in terms of your inner mood, still remaining calm. And if you can stay happy while blowing off steam at the universe, you won't be putting more negativity into your heart box. So, when I find myself feeling angry, I try to get in touch with an inner calm and just "pretend" to be angry. I have found this method very effective in combatting my own symptoms.

People who suffer from PTSD lose so much time to the beast! There is no easy solution; and even though the fire ceremony has helped me more than my numerous counselors were able to do, I have to thank them for the tools and the support I needed at that time in my life, so thank you! I'm not rid of PTSD completely, but between the fire ceremony and Western medicine, I have the most normal life I can have—a better life than I would have had by using only one way or the other.

It is my thought that Western medicine and Original medicine could, and in fact should, work together. I don't understand the hesitancy. The doctors I've talked with protest that our native healing methods can't be tested. But if a billion doses of medicine tea over tens of thousands of years isn't testing, then I don't know what is. Gram explained it like this: Based on past experience, we try a certain tea with people who are ill and see if it works. If it doesn't work because of individual body chemistry, we try something else. This is why we have sometimes twenty herbs for the same purpose— because everyone's chemistry is different.

I have found that there are more than a few ways we can deal with PTSD, and, trust me, on my healing journey I have tried them all.

Answers from Flyingbye

Over the years, due to my exposure to Agent Orange in Vietnam, my health became progressively worse. I found myself falling down more often. Even though I knew that my spiritual growth was important, I became more and more preoccupied with the physical problems brought on by the toxin.

In my search for healing, I was unable to find an Oneida medicine man, so I went to the VA, seeking help. There I met Bob, a Vietnam veteran who counseled other Vietnam vets. He became my therapist. It seems that we might not understand the lessons we get from people when we first meet them until much later.

Bob was of Cree descent, from Canada. He had been adopted in South Dakota by Joe Flyingbye, the great-nephew of the Lakota chief Sitting Bull. Not only was Flyingbye renowned for his medicine work, he was also the head medicine man at Standing Rock Reserve and had proved to be successful in helping people get clear of the toxin Agent Orange.

In 1995 I decided to make the twelve-hour drive to see Flyingbye in Little Eagle, South Dakota, one of the many little towns on the Standing Rock Reserve. As I drove, I thought about what I would ask him: Could he help me with the Agent Orange? And would he teach me about medicine work?

When I arrived in Little Eagle, I got directions to Flyingbye's house from the post office. I walked up to his house in eager anticipation. On the right side of the porch sat a pile of pipestone scrap, left over from making medicine pipes. According to Lakota legend, the pipe was brought to the people by the White Buffalo Calf Woman. I will relate this story to you just as Joe Flyingbye later related it to me:

Two young warriors were out hunting on the prairie. One was a humble man, quiet and peaceful, while the other was more on the arrogant side. He was a show-off, considering himself to be a ladies' man.

Because the tribe had fallen on hard times, the chief had sent out scouts to look for food. These two young men were hunting for buffalo.

As they looked upon the horizon, a white buffalo calf emerged from over a hill, only to disappear down a draw (a small depression in the landscape). When the buffalo reappeared, it had become a young woman dressed in a tanned white dress. She was carrying a sacred bundle, and in the bundle was the sacred pipe. As the woman walked toward the men, they realized how beautiful she was.

The arrogant man said, "I am going to have my way with her."

The humble warrior replied, "Beware; I think this is a sacred being we are seeing."

The first man ignored the warning and walked over to the beautiful young woman. He said something to her that the other man couldn't hear. All of a sudden, a whirlwind engulfed both the arrogant man and the woman in dust, making them invisible.

When the dust cleared, the humble man saw that White Buffalo Calf Woman was standing, not next to the arrogant man, but next to a pile of bones where the man had last stood. Worms and vermin were crawling in the bones. The humble man, fearing for his life, dropped to his knees as the woman came toward him. He asked if there was anything he could do to persuade her to spare his life.

She said, "Rise. I will not hurt you; you have a good heart. Go to the village and tell them that I am coming. You need to prepare a lodge large enough so that everyone in the village will fit in it. I have something for the people."

The humble man agreed. True to his word, he went to the nation and prepared the way for White Buffalo Calf Woman. And, true to *her* word, four days later she came to the village and gathered everyone up in the new lodge. When they were all there, she told them of the sacred pipe—which was the gift she had said she would give the people. She instructed them in the pipe's use, how to make one, and what had to be done to earn one.

After teaching all the ways the pipe could help everyone have a good life, White Buffalo Calf Woman physically offered the pipe to the people. But when they reached for it, she pulled it back. Again she offered them the pipe, and when they reached for it, she withdrew it again. A third time she offered it, only to withdraw it. Finally, on the fourth offering, she let the people have the pipe. But she made them reach for it four times to show the people that not all things come easily and that patience is a virtue. (Flyingbye said that, to honor the way White Buffalo Calf Woman gave the pipe, during a sun dance, when the dancers are on break it is still the custom to offer them water and food four times before releasing these gifts. Most ceremonial acts are done in sets of fours, as in honoring the grandfathers of the four sacred directions.)

Next, White Buffalo Calf Woman gave the people the six other holy rites of the Lakota nation, including the vision quest and the sweat lodge. Immediately afterward, she left the village and began walking up a hill. After walking for a while, the beautiful woman lay down on the ground and rolled over four times. When she got back up, she emerged as a red buffalo calf. She continued farther up the hill and lay down again. She rolled over four more times, and when she arose she was a yellow buffalo calf. Again she walked farther up the hill, lay down, and rolled over four times, and this time she arose as a black buffalo calf. Just before she crested the hill, she lay down and rolled over the last four times. This last time, she ascended as a white buffalo calf. She then mysteriously walked over the hill, not to be seen again.

It has been said that when a white buffalo calf returns, there will be a time of great change and peace upon the earth. And in 1994, Miracle, a white buffalo calf, was indeed born in Janesville, Wisconsin. People came from all over to bring gifts of tobacco and other things. In 2004, Miracle was shot by some white folk who apparently didn't want peace. Nevertheless, let us hope that the predictions of a coming great peace are still true.

That day in 1995, when I first knocked on Flyingbye's front door, it opened ever so slowly. There stood a short Lakota man. He said, "I've been waiting for you, and your answers are yes and no."

"The answers to what?" I asked, confused.

"To your questions," Flyingbye replied. "Yes, I can help you get rid of the Agent Orange. You just need to do thirty-two sweats, and you won't fall down anymore, and the Agent Orange won't kill you.

And no, there is nothing I can teach you about medicine work, since you are better at what you do than I could ever be."

"Oh," I said simply, because he was a renowned medicine man and I was just me. And if you boil things down to their essence, in reality the only one who can truly do healing is the Creator.

Flyingbye went on to say, "I will also have you do a vision quest sometime in the future. It is a ritual where we go on the hill to pray and commune with the Creator. We do this in the hope of getting medicine or answers to questions we may have. But, with your healing power, beware of the two-headed serpent with red eyes as you go up the hill. If you see it and look into those red eyes, you will get a sweet taste in the back of your mouth."

A lingering silence followed. Long pauses are characteristic of the speech of older Lakota people. It is the custom for them to take their time to make sure that one always speaks correctly and truthfully, and it is a sign of respect for the rest of us to be silent and wait for their reply.

After much patience on my part, Flyingbye finally said, "When you taste the really sweet taste in the back of your mouth, it is a sign that you have become the most powerful medicine man ever. You would have the power to point at someone and make them perfectly healthy, or if you don't like them, you could make them dead just as quickly. The power is nice, but there is a price to pay: You would drop several rounds on the spiral to enlightenment, and, believe me, the drop of several lifetimes of work is not a good thing.

"I would like it if you could come and stay out here sometimes, because there aren't a lot of young people who want to know this medicine work," Flyingbye went on. "Come, let us go for a ride; you drive."

On the drive we arrived at the *inipi*—the sweat lodge. "Mitakuye Oyasin [ME-talk-we AH-see]," said Flyingbye as we got out of the car. I asked him what that meant.

"That means," he said, "that we are all relatives, not just we humans. Everything the Creator made—animals, plants, trees, rocks, lakes, and all creation—is part of the circle of life."

"Cool," I said. "My grandmother said the same thing, but a little differently. She told me, 'As people, the Creator loves us. We take care of the Creator's creations as best we can, because everything else the Creator made—along with us—is all part of the Creator's circle, the web of life. We take care of everything because the Creator gave us the responsibility to do so. And always, we are responsible for our own actions.'"

"How old is your grandmother?" Flyingbye asked.

"She crossed over in 1985. She was a wise woman. Tell me more about the vision quest," I urged.

After another one of those long Lakota pauses, he said, "It is where we go for four days." Another outrageously long pause, then, "The hill is where we search for guidance, search for our path, and get medicines. Knowledge of the future may come, too, though it can take years to get your answers."

During Flyingbye's next pause, I remembered one of Gram's stories. Her own great-grandmother had said that, long before the Europeans came, her people had the medicine wheel. It had always been in the four colors—red, yellow, black, and white—before her people were even sure that other races of people shared the earth. Gram's great-grandmother had also told her about the ancient Three Sisters Ceremony, in which her people honored the three sisters of corn, beans, and squash. The purpose of the ceremony was to help the fertility of the seed. But beyond that, it was also to help the fertility of the women. And the ceremonial dance brought all nations together for the good of all; enemies danced side by side. No one knows for sure, Gram had told me, because it happened thousands of years ago. But supposedly, there were red, white, black, and yellow people participating; they were painted each color. When she asked what the colors on the medicine wheel stand for, I replied the four races. "That's right," Gram had confirmed, "I know we don't have black or yellow people here, but someday we will." At the time, living in the boonies outside Spooner, both of us had seen only white and native people. The population of northern Wisconsin was ridiculously white then, and Gram had never been more than several miles from her house.

Flyingbye must have been listening to my thoughts, for next he said, "My Lakota ancestors, including my uncle, Sitting Bull, said that we are all brothers under our skin. We all bleed the same color. But what we as a people didn't realize was that some of the brothers were very greedy. Now we call them *wasichus*. Most people think that means 'white man,' but what it really means is 'eaters of the fat'—people who always take the best for themselves and leave what they don't want for the rest."

It seems that when, several centuries ago, the Lakota people first encountered Caucasians, they were two white trappers who were nearly starving on the prairie. The chief took them back to his lodge to feed them. The meat was first handed to the chief, who took a bite and cut it off, then passed it to the next elder. He, in turn, repeated the action, and then he passed it to one of the trappers. It is said that the trapper then ate the entire piece of meat. Thus, the word *wasichus* came into being.

Among the many wisdoms shared by my teacher Flyingbye, the following is another story he passed on to me.

The chief of the village asked three braves—two very slender boys and a heavyset boy—to go hunting for some deer to eat. The villagers were starving because the buffalo hadn't come in yet on their annual migration. Two of the boys were ambitious and fast. They began their adventure by running to the Missouri River and yelling at the heavyset kid to hurry up. He was a little slower, if not a bit lazy.

The slower boy told the other two to go ahead and he would catch up. Before he was even a third of the way there, the thinner boys had crossed the river and run ahead into the prairie, looking for game. Finally, miles on the other side of the river, they got a deer.

The less enthusiastic boy plodded to the river and crossed it. He then sat down for a snack before he started hunting. While he was eating, a fat buck came to drink from the river. The lazy boy shot it with his bow, gutted it, and dragged it across the Missouri. He pulled it to the top of the bank and set out for the village. Then he decided to get help dragging the deer back because of the bad storm clouds that were gathering.

In the meantime, the other boys were dragging their deer toward the river. It started raining, lightly at first, and then in a cloudburst so hard that they sought shelter. After the rain quit, they continued dragging the deer, arriving at the river just before dark. The river was so high they couldn't get across. They spent the night in a cottonwood grove, damp, hungry, and wet, not being able to get a fire started because of the storm.

It took me a long time to figure out what that story means. Then I realized that its object is to make our brains work. The story means that, sometimes, wanting too much knowledge too fast costs you in the long run. Flyingbye told it to me because, at that younger time in my life, I was a sponge. I wanted to know everything all at once. The story was his way of telling me to go slower.

I stayed with Flyingbye for about a week. While we talked of ceremony, he showed me many herbs that would help to heal those in need. He was a firm believer in the medicine wheel and a firm believer in teaching. He would teach anyone, as long as they were interested. What their color was didn't matter.

The more I talked with him, the more I realized that a whole new dimension of growth was occurring within me. In my own way, during that visit with Flyingbye I had grown to the point of understanding, which proved to me that I was, indeed, on the right path. After absorbing all I could, I set out for my journey back home to Spooner. I was anxious to tell my friend Keith, a fellow 'Nam veteran, about my experience. Keith traveled many times to the reserve with me to learn from Joe Flyingbye, the wise and well-seasoned Lakota medicine man.

The Warriors' Dance

In early November of 1995, my spirit guide came to me in a vision once again. He said, "Let's go for a walk."

"It's dark, and I am sleeping," I replied.

He said, "It is now that we must go."

We left my house, heading north-northwest through the nearby forest. At first, the forest was full of the ordinary trees I was used to seeing; but as we walked, soon the trees became larger, and the traffic noise disappeared. The forest changed from predominantly hardwood to an equal mix of hard and soft woods—mainly Norway spruce, white pine, poplar, and maple.

As we kept moving northwest, the trees changed again, this time to mostly pine in what was a great, old forest. The huge pine trees must have stretched eight to ten feet or more in diameter. The brown needles layering the forest floor gave off a sweet mustiness, mingled with the piney smell of fresh, green needles. The forest was quiet, the fallen needles creating a plush, brown carpet that muffled our footfall—not that I could see the needles in the dark; I just knew.

For a while, the only sound was the needles of the pines as they swished and rattled in the wind. Then, when the wind subsided, I could hear, way in the distance, the pulsing of a big dance drum. But when the wind picked back up, all I could hear again was the breeze whispering through the needles.

And so, on we walked.

Again and again the wind would build and soften. Each time it subsided, I could hear the drum playing a bit louder. Eventually, the drumming became constant, in spite of the whispering pine needles.

Finally, the deep forest opened onto a huge, circular meadow, seven or eight hundred yards wide. In the moonlight, I could see an enclosure, or arena, which was about three hundred feet around. It had a sloping roof and twelve-foot-high cedar walls.

As my spirit guide and I crossed the meadow and approached the arena, the drumming became ever louder. The doorway on the south side of the arena was covered with woven cedar, blocking our entrance. So we walked sunwise (clockwise) until we reached the east side. Again, cedar covered the door, and the same was true of the north door. The west door was the only open entrance. As we approached it, two native men dressed in their finest quilled ceremonial attire were smudging people with sage. Huge abalone shells held the burning sage, and the men wafted the smoke toward us with eagle-wing fans.

Waiting at the door to be smudged, I saw perhaps two thousand women under the arena roof. They stood side by side in beautiful leather dresses adorned with eagle feathers. Some were wearing red plumes; others wore yellow, white, or blue. Their feathers made an awe-inspiring rainbow of color when they flitted in the wind as the women did their sidestep dance.

Eight groups of men danced around eight fires that encircled the arena space. The fires faced in eight directions: the four cardinal directions of north, south, east, and west, and the four secondary directions of northeast, northwest, southeast, and southwest. The dancing was completely uninhibited and much more primal than what you would see at powwows today.

After my spirit guide and I were smudged, we entered the arena, excusing ourselves as we passed through the women. I was looking at a free, happy people who were truly wild. There was no tameness about them. When we walked up to the first fire to dance, I noticed that the warriors wore flint axes as well as knives of agate and flint stone in quilled sheaths. There was no metal of any sort among these folks.

As we danced with the men, I looked at the circle of women. Unlike the men, they were dancing in place, always facing forward. On certain drumbeats, they would do a half-step to the left, maintaining their forward positions.

I was trying to absorb everything at once. I was excited, yet overwhelmed at having been given the great honor of seeing these people dancing, as no one else has seen for the last thousand years or so.

"Overwhelmed?" asked my guide. "Why now? What were you looking for at this time in your life?"

I realized that I was looking for reassurance that I was on the right path. Was the scene before me difficult to believe, or was it a kind of confirmation? I quickly came to the conclusion that it was definitely a confirmation.

As we danced at the second fire, I noticed seven or eight men playing and singing around the drum. They, too, were each completely unique and yet somehow similar. They were strong, youthful warriors, though some were a bit older.

Still dancing, I glimpsed the huge drum. Even in the dim light of the moon and the fires, the painted colors glowed brightly. Four bent black sticks surrounded the drum, and, as I danced, it appeared to float in midair. It was moving rhythmically with the beats. Each time the men beat on the drum, the drum bounced up to meet the down beat.

We moved on to the next fire, and the next, dancing with these proud and beautiful people. I felt most comfortable at the fire that faced southwest, but I had no idea why. When we had danced our way back to where we had started, we walked over to the drummers.

In the flickering firelight, I couldn't understand the significance of the bent sticks, which resembled upside-down Js. Moving close enough to see the symbol on the drum face, I saw that it looked like two cursive capital Ts written in bright black. Each was a mirror image of the other. Three red balls, an inch and a half in diameter, were placed near the first T. One was on the bottom left and two were on the right top of the T. The red balls on the opposite T were placed in a reverse mirror image. The drum seemed to float as the players beat on it and sang their old songs. As I watched, I started to feel dizzy. I awoke to find myself sitting on the edge of my bed and quickly jotted down some notes so I wouldn't forget any part of this sensational experience.

The next morning, I called my friend Joe Flyingbye, with whom I had studied ceremony and herbal medicine for several years, and told him the story of my dream vision. When I asked what kind of dance I had witnessed, he explained that it wasn't Lakota, because the Lakota do not dance at night. He said, "I know many chiefs and holy men, and I will find out what kind of dance that is."

December went by, then January and February. On the ninth of March, 1996, I received Flyingbye's long-awaited call. He said, "The vision you had was of a Warrior Dance of the Anishinabe."

This news startled me. *Anishinabe* means "first" or "original people." Traditionally, the Anishinabe are considered to have formed the first nation and are thought of as the "true people."

Flyingbye went on, "I want you to call Robert [Tomaywashing], the chief of the Anishinabe tribe at Dog Creek Reserve. It's two hundred and fifty miles northwest of Winnipeg in Canada."

When Robert answered the phone, I said, "This is Russell FourEagles, and I had a vision." Right away I told him that I was of German and Norwegian as well as Anishinabe and Oneida descent, with pale skin and blue eyes. He said that was okay: he himself—a chief—has blond hair and blue eyes. As I related the story of my vision, he said, "I am most interested in the drum. Those symbols you describe are on our *own* drum, here on the reserve, and no white man has seen it since 1867, when the Canadian government outlawed everything native. So our people hid it."

"Where did they hide it?" I asked.

"In the attic of the church. If anything needed to be stored or moved from there, the white people wouldn't do it; our people would. So our drum has been safe. For one hundred and twenty-nine years, no white man has seen it. But you have described it exactly. I think you need to come to our Warrior Dance at the end of next month."

The third week in April, I drove to Dog Creek. Heavy rain and flooding had closed down some of the roads, but eventually I made it. I arrived in the evening and introduced myself to Robert. He had many questions: "Who is your warrior? What clan are you from? What are your colors? Are you going to dance as a warrior?"

"I don't know," I said. "But I am going to the drum circle, and I will pray until I get an answer from the Creator."

The drum circle was a circular, overhead structure supported by a dozen or so eight-foot-tall beams. As I stood in its center with my sleeping bag over my shoulders, watching the night sky, I saw the moon appear inside the roofless frame. Thin, fast-moving clouds obscured the moon's surface. The clouds were crossing the sky at sixty miles per hour, moving much faster here in the northern plains than they did in the hills of Wisconsin.

Early in the evening, cars began arriving. People unloaded their vehicles and set up their tents. One area was for the warriors and another for the spectators. The dance and the four sweat lodges were located in two separate areas. After ten o'clock, it quieted down.

I prayed and prayed to the Creator, asking, "What is it you want me to do?" As I prayed, waiting for an answer, through the center of the drum circle I watched the moon progress slowly across the sky. The clouds sped by, sometimes thicker, sometimes thinner. As early morning approached, the faintest red line creased the eastern horizon. I knew I was running out of time. I would soon have to give Robert an answer. Finally, I prayed to the Creator, "If you won't answer me directly, would you please give me a sign?"

Masked by the clouds, the glowing orb of the moon was about to hit the edge of the drum circle frame. Beneath the clouds, four stars appeared. At first, I didn't recognize them. But then it dawned on me that these were the same stars as the ones on the patch I had worn in the Vietnam War. They formed the Southern Cross of the Americal Division. The bright spot of the moon was inside the drum circle, and the Southern Cross was near the moon but *outside* the circle. I could identify with the stars, which, being outside, signified a supporting role.

When Robert asked if I had gotten an answer to my prayers, I answered, "Yes, I am going to be a *scabae* (helper)."

"Then are you ready to start? I know you've been awake all night, but we only have five days to prepare for the dance. Take the tractor and trailer and cut spruce boughs for the arena," he said.

"Isn't it supposed to be cedar?" I asked.

"Yes, but that was before the government cut and sold all the cedar to the US companies. Now what cedar we have is saved for the west door and its roof."

With four or five other men I loaded boughs into the huge chopper box with eight-foot-high walls. One older guy was on the chainsaw, and he also drove the tractor. It took a couple of hours to load the box and get it back to the arena. While we were gone, a group of people had started putting up the twelve-foot uprights and mounted the top rail of the arena. This was larger than the drum circle and would enclose it.

We delivered the boughs and headed back to the woods with an empty wagon. The land on this reserve was flat but higher than lowland. Willows and scrub pine grew there, typical of a swamp. But the ground was just high enough above water level to support a few hardwoods. Somehow, it was possible to drive a truck on it without the wheels sinking in.

As we got back to the woods, a light rain began, coating everything with slime. We kept working and went to another area, where the man sawing dropped five or six seventy- to one-hundred-foot-high spruce. He cut off the limbs, and we loaded the boughs into the tall-sided wagon.

After we finished the arena, Robert asked if a few of us would cut firewood for the sweat lodges and the fires. We soon started the sacred fire, which had to keep burning throughout the dancing, day and night.

That afternoon, I was a fire-tender at the women's sweat lodge, so I built the platform and asked the woman in charge how many rocks she wanted. "Eighteen," she replied. I gathered the rocks, piled the wood, and started the fire. I worked eagerly so that it would be ready for the dance at six o'clock. I hadn't eaten or drunk anything for twenty-four hours before the dance began. This was because I chose to fast with the warriors in their support.

After the sweat was over, I started the seven other fires, keeping them going until the dance started. A half hour before the dance began, the drummers brought the drum into the center.

When I saw it, my hair stood on end. On it was painted the exact same pattern of symbols—with the cursive Ts and red balls—that I had seen in my vision. I now understood the bent sticks. They had a thin piece of sinew on them, and the sinew was tied to the drum; but in the dim firelight of the vision, I hadn't seen the sinew. Over hundreds of years, the weight of the drum had naturally bent the sticks. One other difference from the vision was that the symbols on this drum, while still clear, now looked faded, as if they had been drummed on for hundreds of years. I asked Robert how old the drum was. He said no one knows for sure, as the exact date has faded into the past. But he had heard it was between five and six hundred years old or more.

When the drumming began, in the flickering firelight the drum appeared to float, just as it had in my vision. Also as in my vision, there were eight fires in the eight directions. Sometime after the dance, Robert explained that each direction was assigned to a clan. The Moose Clan was at the north fire, the Bear Clan at the east, the Deer Clan at the south, and the Elk Clan at the west. In terms of secondary directions, the Turtle Clan was at the northeast fire, the

Mink at the southeast, the Eagle at the southwest, and the Crane at the northwest. But, Robert said, that had only been his way of doing it; who was where depended on which clans showed up.

I danced with the warriors at each of the fires. They appeared so similar to what I had seen in the vision, and again I noticed how each dancer was yet an individual, unique in his own way. The dance went on without a hitch.

At midnight, the dancing stopped and the warriors retired to pray and sleep. I asked Robert if I should watch the sacred fire, but he explained that he had asked someone else to do it. I said I would stay up with the other man, anyway. It was a good thing I did, since the fire tender fell asleep about three o'clock in the morning. I dutifully kept the fire going until people were up and around. Then Robert asked me to cut a couple more loads of wood for the sweat lodges and the arena.

Afterward, I got the sweat lodge ready for the next sweat and, with the help of a few others, the clan fires going in preparation for the dance. We fed the fires, occasionally dancing with different fires or clans.

After the dancing was over, I was sitting by the sacred (east) fire when Robert found me.

"I know you have been awake for three days and nights. I hate to ask you to watch the sacred fire, but I can't find anyone else to do it."

"I don't mind," I replied, and for the second night I watched the fire until the people stirred. The routine was similar to the one for my bimonthly sweat lodges at home: cut wood; clean the lodge; gather rock; feed the guests; and get the fires built up, ready for the next dance.

In the afternoon, a piercing ceremony was held. Volunteers have their skin cut and pegs inserted through the cuts so that they can be tethered with ropes. The purpose of this ritual is to have a few suffer for the many, thus protecting the tribe as a whole. In a way, this ceremony could be likened to the suffering Jesus did so that his people wouldn't have to.

The appointed helpers laid down Robert, the chief. On each side of his back they made two cuts, about two inches apart and one inch long, through which a chokecherry peg was inserted under the skin. A rope had been split into two strands with loops at the ends. The men tied the end of each strand to one of the pegs in Robert's back. To the other end of the rope they attached a dozen buffalo skulls that Robert was to pull.

In fulfillment of the ritual, Robert stood up, leaned against the thongs and started pulling the skulls. Soon, he was running around the arena. He made it all the way to his beginning point. Then, four or five young girls got on top of the skulls and Robert took off again, this time for about twenty yards. The first peg pulled through his skin, and then the other broke and released him, causing him to fall.

One of the medicine men went to him, said prayers, cut off the loose flaps of skin, and put tobacco on his cuts. When Robert got up, there was a lot of hooting and hollering.

During the ceremony a few women also tethered. But unlike the men—who, other than Robert, tethered to their chests—the women tethered to the tops of their shoulders. A young boy of eleven or twelve, with blonde hair and blue eyes, lay down and was cut and tethered. He broke on his first pull.

After that night's dance, Robert asked again if I could watch the fire. "No problem," I answered. Again I kept the sacred fire going, prayed, and talked to people now and again as they came and sat by the fire.

In the early morning, I noticed a tendril of smoke coming from the southwest fire. It was soon joined by three more tendrils, all dancing around each other like a loose braid. My gaze returned to the sacred fire. When I looked back at the Eagle Clan fire, five warriors were dancing, backed by seven others. The twelve warriors were fierce-looking men with painted faces in patterns of black and white. The upper face of some was black, from the center line of the nose up to the hairline, with the lower part of the face white. Some were painted in the opposite way. The faces of others were split with black and white paint right and left, down the center of the nose from hairline to throat. Still others had vertical or horizontal black and white bands. Though ferocious-looking, these *jimaganish* (warriors) conveyed an innate beauty in the simple patterns of the black and white they wore.

As they danced, they looked at me, and I became startled. My first thought was that no one had told me there was to be an early morning dance. Then I remembered that, in the ceremony, warriors don't *have* a morning dance. So what was happening?

I then thought that I must have fallen asleep at the sacred fire—I must be dreaming. I decided that if, in fact, this was a dream, it would be possible to touch the fire without it harming me. I reached out my right hand, turned it over, and gingerly touched the back of my wrist to the red-hot coal. Much to my surprise, it hurt like hell; I instantly developed a dime-size blister on my wrist. To this day, the skin there is redder than the skin around it. So what I was seeing wasn't a dream.

"Aho," I thought. "These are spirit warriors." To see spirits and yet still be in the waking world where a hand can burn does sometimes happen at native ceremonies.

The spirit warriors were all dressed in white buckskin with long fringe on the leggings and sleeves. I noticed that, on one arm and the opposite leg, they wore black diamonds. Yellow light emanated from the border between the black of the diamonds and the white of the buckskin. On the other limbs, the warriors had black lightning symbols with the same yellow light radiating where the black met the white. The bright glow reminded me of dyed ostrich plumes waving in the breeze; but it was an actual *light*, and not anything material, that danced around the designs. And it came from *inside* the dancers—it was their inner energy made visible.

I then realized that the Creator was showing me my clan on the Anishinabe side of my family and that I must offer a handful of tobacco to say thank you. I was sure that after I put the tobacco on the fire, the vision would be gone.

Sure enough, as I prayed and offered the tobacco, a huge ball of smoke rose from the fire and blocked my view of the dancing warriors. But after the smoke cleared, I was shocked to see the warriors still dancing. They must have something more to tell me, but what was it?

"Are those my colors?" I asked. They simply smiled at me, fading as they danced. Soon I could see the arena right through them, and they faded away to nothing. After they were gone, within my head I heard, "My brother, you are ready to go on a vision quest [*Hanblecheya*]."

Vision Quest

The morning after my vision of the dancing warriors, I told Robert what the spirits had said. He told me that it is very important to do as you are instructed; otherwise, the spirits will stop giving you things. By noon I had found a man to take my place as the tender for the women's sweat. I said my goodbyes, packed up my car, and headed home to make some arrangements. It was time to follow my vision quest. I would be going up to Elkhorn Butte.

On the way home from Manitoba, I stopped to see some friends just south of Grantsburg, Wisconsin. These friends and I would sometimes sweat together. I wanted to tell them of my plans for my vision quest. One of them, Chris, was a large man, standing six-feet-five and weighing about 280 pounds. He confided in me that he, too, was thinking about going on a quest, and so we decided to go together. I went home, made my calls, and prepared for our journey.

The next day, Chris and I were in his truck, heading for the Standing Rock Reserve in South Dakota. I had been going to Standing Rock since 1990, when I had sought help from Flyingbye for my health problems brought on by Agent Orange.

We pulled into the town of Mobridge, South Dakota, at about four o'clock in the morning, and stopped at a restaurant. I noticed a table of four young cowboys, about twenty-five years old, sipping on mugs of hot, steamy coffee. As Chris and I drank our coffee, we talked about how the next four days would play out.

Chris said, "We should be at the reserve by about seven-thirty. Then we will see Flyingbye and find some guys to man the fire for the sweat. We will go on the mountain and be done on the following Friday."

By the "mountain," Chris was referring to Elkhorn Butte, traditionally the site for vision quests on the Standing Rock Reserve. It was more commonly called the "hill." On the first day of the quest, we would do the first half of our sweat in the lodge on the flat land and then go on the hill. We would be on the hill for four days before going back to the lodge for the second half of the sweat.

When Chris headed for the bathroom, one of the cowboys approached our table and informed me that I should cut my long black hair because it made me look like a "prairie nigger."

I calmly responded that, although I am from Wisconsin, I supposed I *was* a prairie nigger. But what did he have against people who could speak two or three languages?

"Can you?" I asked.

"No," he said. People in South Dakota were used to Indians who would kowtow and not talk back. I relayed that I had killed a lot of people in Vietnam and I considered any one of those guys to be much better than the cowboy was. At that point I invited him to leave—and, to my surprise, he and the rest of his friends all left.

Chris and I stuck around for a bit longer and then headed back out to the open road. We had to cross the Missouri River Bridge, which is about a mile long, plus the approaches. While we were driving, I could hear a young girl crying.

"Chris, do you hear that?"

"Yes, it's a girl of fifteen who was brutally raped and murdered under the bridge."

"How come no one has helped her?"

"What do you mean?" Chris asked.

"How come no one has helped her cross over?"

"I don't know."

"We will have to do that on our way back home; do you agree?"

"Yes, I guess somebody should, since she has been crying for years," Chris said. After we got across the bridge and into Standing Rock Reserve, the hair on my head finally settled down.

When we finally arrived at our destination, we learned that one of the elders had died. That would keep Flyingbye busy for a couple of days; as the medicine man, he was in charge of the funeral to be held up in northern Standing Rock. In the meantime, we went to camp by the *inipi* (sweat lodge). Upon arrival at the lodge, we noticed there was no wood for the sweat. Finding wood would take two days, so we settled in and got busy. The wood would be used in an outside fire pit to heat the rocks. When the rocks were hot enough for a sweat, they would be carried into the lodge using antler prongs.

On the third day, Chris said, "If we don't get to go on the mountain tomorrow, I'm going to be pissed."

"Chris," I said, "remember that, next to the Sun Dance, this vision quest is the Lakota people's most sacred ceremony, so be careful how you talk. You don't want to have trouble on the hill."

"I am not going to have any trouble on the hill. It's just that they work so much on Indian time."

"Need you be reminded of where we are?" I asked.

"No," he replied, in a resigned tone.

After our conversation, three young Lakota guys stopped by the inipi and asked what we were doing. We told them we were going on the hill. Looking over our things, they spotted the four Iroquois masks I had made modeled on the ones my spirit guide had given me in a vision. I was to hang them in the cardinal directions in the arena that would be my protection for the four days I was on my quest.

"What are those things?" asked one of the young men, Ben.

"They're sacred masks my spirit guide gave me to protect me from the Little People while I'm on the hill."

The "Little People" are what the Oneida call nature spirits or fairies. They like to harass people who are in sacred places, and they try to break a person's spirit so that he can't finish his quest and find out what lessons the Creator has for him. If the Little People succeed in this meanness, they become big men in their little tribe.

"You shouldn't be using those masks on a *Lakota* vision quest!" said Ben, rather sternly.

"What makes you say that?" I asked.

"Because that is not how we do it out here."

"I'll tell you what: let's go talk to Grandfather Flyingbye."

"Okay, let's do it."

Chris, Ben, and I hopped in the car and drove to Joe Flyingbye's house. He was now back from conducting the funeral and should be available to talk. "What do you fellows want?" he asked when he opened his door.

Ben blurted out, "He's not doing the vision quest right!"

"Oh, really? What is he doing wrong?" asked Joe.

"He has got some silly-ass wooden masks he wants to take with him up on the hill."

"Do you know why?"

"Not exactly. He said something about his spirit guide."

"Hmmm." After another of Joe's long pauses that I was getting used to, he asked me, "Why are you taking those masks up on the hill?"

"Back home my spirit guide took me on a vision quest and said to use them, as they would keep the Little People from harassing me while on quest."

"So these masks came from spirit, then?" asked Joe. When I said yes, Flyingbye turned to Ben.

"Ben, whenever spirit brings you something for a sacred purpose and you don't use it, then you will likely not be given anything else, as spirit will think you don't need it and find someone else who does. So enough about there being only one way to do things—especially sacred things, which developed as they did by spirit guiding many different people in how to live better. Don't worry about how other people do their vision quest; just worry about how you will do your own." With that lesson from Flyingbye, we drove back to the sweat lodge, where Chris and I dropped Ben off with his friends.

On Thursday, four days after Chris and I had arrived, we finally had enough wood to make a fire in the outside fire pit for the first half of the sweat—the purification ceremony, which would help prepare us for the vision quest. During this part of the sweat we did two "doors," or rounds, of prayers. Each round is done facing one of the four cardinal directions. After we came back from the hill, we would do the remaining two doors, completing the quest.

When Chris and I finished the second door, Flyingbye—who was with us in the lodge—asked us to think about why we were going on the hill. I said, "I'm going to pray for the people and for my wife to get a voice. After twenty-five years of marriage, we don't seem to have a lot to talk about. Maybe I can find out what is on her mind."

"Well, son," Flyingbye said, "be careful what you wish for, as you may very well get it."

Aside from the sacred Iroquois masks, I had brought several other things to help me on the vision quest. This is how I came to have them:

About a year earlier, in the spring of 1995, Joe Flyingbye's sons— Alan and Bob—had stopped by my house in Wisconsin. Both are medicine men trained by their father. They had come to instruct me in general for any vision quest I would eventually take.

Bob said, "I think you should start preparing for a quest now."

"How do I do that?" I asked.

"First you have to make prayer ties for your 'surround,' or arena. You then have to get a new star quilt that has never been used. You will also need a new, never-used knife. Finally, you will need a fresh buffalo skull; and be sure, if you get one from a slaughterhouse, that the skull isn't broken between the eyes. As you gather these things, be certain to do your tobacco prayers, and place the tobacco on the ground."

Following instructions, I gathered chensasa (chen-sha-sha), sinew from venison, and tobacco and set about making the ties, which are small pouches containing prayers. Chensasa is a sacred tobacco from the inner bark of red willow—or, in European terms, red osier (dogwood). First I mixed the chensasa 25/75 with the tobacco, doing my protection prayers. Then I took a one-inch-square of red cloth and laid it flat in one hand while holding up a pinch of tobacco with the other. I said four prayers to the Creator for each tie, asking for protection from the elements, protection from wild animals, and protection from confused spirits. And I asked the Creator to hear my prayers, that they might be answered.

Having done the prayers, I placed the tobacco in the middle of the square of cloth and pulled up the four corners, tying them with one long piece of sinew. In this way I made a continuous line of prayer ties on the single strand of sinew every half inch. I continued until I had 270 ties, the number Bob specified. He had also said to make two strands of twelve ties each for the small sticks that I was to place by the buffalo skull.

"The ties will be wound and wound around the sticks until they look somewhat like a cattail," he told me.

I had to search long and hard for a never-used star quilt. Finally I found a woman in the Ojibwa reserve near Hayward, Wisconsin, who makes them. One hundred seventy dollars later, I owned my first star quilt.

To obtain the buffalo skull I went to a ranch. I needed a fresh skull as a sacred symbol of the life of the Lakota people, who were sustained by the buffalo in many ways. While there, I asked if I could have a couple of buffalo ribs. With a rib, I made a new knife. The knife was for protection—not from predators or men, but from storms. If the *Waniggi* (WA nee gee; Thunder Beings) came while I was on my quest, I could cut the clouds with the knife so that they would pass on each side of wherever I was.

It took two months or more to gather all the sacred objects that I needed for the quest. It took so long, in fact, that by the time I was ready, it was too late to do a quest that fall. It was then that I had had the vision of the Anishinabe Warrior's Dance and gone to Manitoba.

Now here I was at last on the Standing Rock Reserve in South Dakota, doing the vision quest with Chris. The day before the sweat, I asked Adam to be my helper, and he agreed. People doing this ritual need helpers, part of the reason being that the fire in the sweat lodge has to stay lit for the whole time the vision seeker is on the hill. It is our belief that, if the fire goes out, something bad can happen. What, you ask? I don't know, as I never heard of that happening, even during bad rains.

After the first half of the sweat, Adam wrapped us in our star quilts so tightly that we had to peek through a little slit to see to walk. When you are in a sacred space like that, it is imperative to be completely covered, because to be seen by any one impure could mess with your quest.

With us we had our buffalo skulls, our tobacco, our never-used knives, and our tobacco prayer ties for protection. And, of course, we each had a medicine pipe, otherwise known as a *chenunpa* in Lakota, or *calumet* in my language. I didn't have a pipe of my own, so Adam allowed me to borrow his. Carrying a pipe is a huge responsibility. When you are a pipe-carrier, your life becomes the Creator's, not your own.

Adam instructed me on how to fill the pipe with the sacred tobacco, chensasa, covered with sage. Flyingbye put a buffalo-fat wax seal on top of the mixture, impressed with some kind of sacred symbol. He also instructed us to remember that, if a big storm came up, we should use the knife to cut the clouds so that they would go around us. He added that at most times when you are on a hill, your struggles are your own, so face them. If all else fails, pray harder.

Most of the struggles we have to face we make so much more of than they truly are. We can face things best by walking in love and not fear. So often we make unfounded assumptions. We expend much more energy worrying needlessly than it would take to solve the problem. It especially helps to remember that all things are perfect in the Creator's way. How often have we worried tremendously over something, only to realize later, in hindsight, that it turned out perfectly? Thus, all that worry was for nothing.

Take, for instance, the child who has a terrible home life. How does he begin to face things? All things come about in the Creator's time. We know not what lessons the child needs, because we cannot walk his journey for him. I myself had a pretty hard home life when I was living with my family. Being the middle child, I was about ten when my dad gave me the job of splitting the wood to heat the house. This was a huge responsibility, in that our family's warmth for the entire winter depended solely on me. Because the job was mine alone, without help, some people thought my dad was being too hard on me. But I must admit that he was always fair. He would bring up a pile of wood in the trailer behind the tractor, and, when I was finished chopping it, I was free to go play or do whatever my heart desired (within the rules, of course).

Looking back now, I know I wouldn't have traded that life for any cushy one. It is one of the many things that made me who I am today. When young children are ready to deal with a hard life, they will be able to. And the parents—just as my dad did—always seem to know when the time is right. So, if the children keep up with their prayers and truly listen to their inner voice, they will be just fine—especially if they follow Flyingbye's advice: if all else fails, pray harder.

Elkhorn Butte, the site of the quest, has two hills: one lower and the other higher by forty or fifty feet. Chris, Adam, and I were nearing the top of the lower hill when Adam said, "Which one of you wants to stay here?"

Chris answered, "I want the very top."

"Here is fine with me," I said.

I took my buffalo skull, prayer ties, and pipe out of the truck. I also removed the chokecherry branches that Adam had cut for me. About five to six feet long, these branches would make the surround in which I would stay during my quest. The leaves were left on the branches to protect me at least somewhat from sunburn.

Adam did a prayer for a good quest and then made holes for the branches with a long steel bar and put the branches in the ground. He set one pole in each of the cardinal directions and a fifth pole to the side of the east one to make a doorway. Then he set the buffalo skull facing east and instructed me to stick the knife into the ground with the blade facing away from the skull. He hung the four Iroquois masks on the poles for protection from the Little People. When my spirit guide had taken me on quest in a vision, he had said to watch for the Little People but that they would not come any closer than twenty to twenty-five feet of the masks.

After I entered the surround, I would not come out for three or four days. I had stopped eating two days before the sweat, because I didn't want to have to go to the bathroom. I knew that, as long as I stayed inside my prayer ties, I would be safe.

Still praying, Adam wrapped two sticks with some of the prayer ties and placed the sticks near the skull. Then he did the last step of stringing the ties all the way around my surround, including between the two poles that made the doorway, at three different levels. This made three strings of protection around me, with the door closed off.

When Adam was finished, he wished me good luck and said he would see me the next day. He and Chris disappeared up the higher hill. I stood there holding the borrowed pipe and praying. By the time Adam drove down the hill it was dusk, and his headlights were on. As it got darker, the temperature started to drop. I soon felt the cold. I heard a noise behind me, from the west. When I turned, I saw what looked like prairie dogs walking up the hill on their hind legs. But they came only within twenty-five feet or so from one of the masks. They soon went back down the hill. They approached again from the south and then from the east, each time stopping before reaching a mask, only to depart back down the hill. After the mask of the north confronted them, they headed up the hill in the direction of Chris. Darn if they didn't look like eighteen-inch-high people! I attributed that to the glow of dusk and not having had anything to eat for two days.

The darker it got, the colder I got. For a long period of time, I prayed and watched frost work toward the surround. About seven-thirty or eight o'clock (just a guess; I had no watch), Chris started screaming. He continued doing so off and on all night. I guess his spirit guide hadn't given him any masks to protect himself with.

The wind picked up. Sometimes I heard drumming coming from the top of the hill and then an occasional scream. I was wet from the sweat, or at least my cotton shorts were. The colder it got, the more I shivered and the more screams I heard. I also heard the great drum of the reserve. As I prayed, I wondered why they were dancing down below, in Little Eagle. I was now freezing to death, so I sat to conserve heat. The frost came into my surround. I was telling the Creator that I didn't think I could do what was asked of me, when a man walked over to me. I offered him my pipe as he asked, "What's the matter?"

"I am freezing to death," I stuttered.

He said, "You know what you have to do," and turned and walked away, displaying long brown hair grown down to his hips.

I was trying to think, but it wasn't easy while shivering from the cold. Then it came to me: my wet shorts were like ice on my skin. So I took them off and became instantly warmer. I stood there and started praying harder. As I prayed, I warmed, and as I warmed, the frost moved farther out, toward the perimeter of my ties. Miraculously, it stayed out the rest of the night. This was, in part, because of my prayers. Also, credit is due to a spirit lady who came up as I was praying and smiled at me. She didn't say anything, but there was such love and heat in the beautiful woman's smile!

Later, as I prayed, I saw a falling star, and I instantly knew that I would be okay. You can't begin to fathom the vastness of the universe until you stand on top of a butte in central South Dakota on a clear, cold night. If you happen to see a night sky without boundaries, its multitude of stars appearing so big and so close up, then maybe—and only maybe—you will be able to somewhat understand the vastness I experienced those many years ago.

It was breaking day, and I was warming up, when I saw some jackrabbits running this way and that through the valley. Then I began to pray. Soon I heard a voice behind me say, "I can't take this. I'm going to walk back to Little Eagle." I wasn't sure if it was a spirit or Chris. I kept praying. I couldn't imagine walking twelve or fifteen miles through the scrub, barefoot.

By nine o'clock in the morning it was getting warmer. I was starving, but soon the sensation went away, as it continued to do whenever I felt hunger over the next three days.

Sometime later that first morning, Adam came to find out how I was doing.

"I'm fine, although it was a struggle at first," I said.

"We were concerned in town, because it got down to eighteen degrees last night. You didn't get frostbite, did you?"

"No," I replied. "What kind of dance were the people doing in Little Eagle?"

Adam replied that there had been no dance.

"Wasn't there a drum group practicing in town or by the lodge?"

"No again," he said. "Those were spirit drummers you heard. See you sometime tomorrow." He disappeared as quietly as a ghost.

By noon it was actually hot—hot enough to burn blisters on the tops of my feet. I was beginning to wonder which was worse, the cold or the heat. But then I realized it was perfect as it was, even though I suffered most of the day under the scorching sun. Either I could cover my head with shade, or I could cover my feet, but not both. So I alternated, back and forth, trying to keep the blisters on my feet from getting too big and my lips from getting too chapped.

I became so thirsty when it got hot. I hadn't had a drink of water for four days, and my lips were becoming badly sunburned. But then, after being thirsty all this time, in a flash of insight I thought, "You have water stones in your medicine bag, dummy!" I had my medicine bag with me, but I had forgotten about the six stones I had found underwater in a lake in Manitoba. I knew them for water stones because they had been floating six inches up from the lake floor, not all the way on the bottom as they should have been.

How stupid, I thought. So I took one stone and put it in my mouth. Instantly, I felt like I had a half gallon of water out of it, and my thirst was satisfied for hours. From then on, whenever I got thirsty I put another stone in my mouth. I was able to finish the entire quest without thirst by switching stones whenever I needed them.

I spent the rest of the day praying and trying to stay cool. Finally, I asked the Creator for a little breeze. Soon a light breeze came up, and it was good. The day progressed uneventfully. But Flyingbye had told me to watch everything, because you never know. Shortly after sunset, the breeze quit, but it continued to stay warm.

As I prayed, I heard something like the buzz I have had in my ear ever since I was in Vietnam. Only now, it was getting louder. Soon I knew what it was: millions of mosquitoes. It became very hard to ignore them, and I found myself rubbing my arms and legs so much that they were turning red with my blood. For more than an hour I did more sweating than praying. I tried to wrap my star quilt tighter around myself, but even the inside of the blanket was getting red streaks.

Finally, I remembered Flyingbye telling me that sometimes, when trying to cross a river, it is easier to swim with the current than to fight it. So I said to the mosquitoes, "I am here. Come drink your fill; you are my relatives, so come drink. Help yourselves." As I dropped my star quilt to the ground, amazingly, my brothers the mosquitoes left me for the rest of my quest. Not only that, but even now, ten years later, the mosquitoes leave me alone. It drives my wife crazy that I don't have to use mosquito repellent.

Again I prayed the night away. At dawn, a big red buffalo came to me, dropped a huge ball of sage in my arena, and said, "Take this message to the east and burn it."

"What does it say?"

"You will know when you burn it."

In a vision I headed east, toward the valley that is east of Elkhorn. When I reached the place where I could view the valley, I saw that it was full of dust. And in that dust, all I could see to the south, east, and north were buffalo. I went into the valley and picked my way through the buffalo with my ball of sage. It was easy at first, as there was space around each buffalo. But it grew steadily harder to move as I walked farther into the herd, because soon their bodies were tight together.

Finally, raising my voice so as to be heard above all the bellowing buffalo, I screamed, "I can't do this thing you ask of me! I am but a weak, pitiful man. I can't get through it."

Then, in the fog of the dust, I saw the huge red buffalo stepping easily over the backs of the others.

When he got to me, he said, "Get on my back." He lowered his head so that I could get ahold of his horn, and then he hoisted me up. We soon arrived on the east side of the valley, where he let me down.

I climbed to the top of the hill on that side of the valley and lit the sage. As the sage smoked, a message came out of it: All people are to come together: red, yellow, black, and white. If we want to survive as a species, now more than ever we must work together for the good of all.

I went back down, crossed the valley, and eventually found myself back at the surround, standing where I had started. With my pipe and my prayers, I was beginning to think—no, I was coming to *know*—that anything was possible while on a vision quest.

On the third or fourth morning, just after daylight, I watched a coyote far across the valley run toward me. It turned back at a bit of an angle, then toward me, and then back at an angle, and again toward me, a third time. I stood many minutes staring at the coyote's zigzag trail as it came toward me and moved away. Suddenly a yellow light that looked just like a lightning bolt came from the ground. I recognized it as the design I had seen in Manitoba at the Warrior's Dance. As I stood praying, I saw four eagles flying toward Elkhorn.

When they reached me, they made four circles over me. Then, one after another, they headed for Little Eagle in the distance.

On the morning of the fourth day, Adam arrived and said prayers to release me. He opened up the surround and asked if there were things I wanted to keep from the quest.

"Yes," I said. "I want the knife to go to Tunkasila (Grandfather Flyingbye). I promised the skull to someone going on quest back in Wisconsin. And I want to keep the four sacred Iroquois masks that my spirit guide gave me in a vision."

As I walked down the hill, four turtle shells appeared fifteen feet in front of my face. They were spinning clockwise, each one with a white spot in the middle of it. All four of them started spinning around each other and formed a single disc with a circular white band. When they stopped spinning, I saw that they made a war shield with four white eagle heads, each facing one of the sacred directions. Then the vision ended.

By the way, I never did see the two-headed serpent with red eyes that Flyingbye had warned me about. When he first told me about it, I wasn't really sure what it meant. However, as I studied with him, I became aware that it was the dark-side energy, similar to Satan in Christianity, but not entirely.

We all know that there is no bad medicine, as all medicine comes from the Creator. There is only good medicine used in bad ways. People who use good medicine in bad ways, in essence, are trying to take power away from the Creator. Doing that always comes back to haunt them. But the Creator gave us all free will; no one can take that away.

Learning My Own Lessons about Rocks

A client once asked me why I had stone spheres under the healing table. Although Grandma knew about the power of these stones, she had only partially taught me about them. One thing she said is that stones haven't been used in healings since cloth became readily available in the 1800s. Obviously cloth was easier to carry around for the fire ceremony than stones were (although Gram did carry a few small ones). And when my spirit guide in the woods had pointed out the rock artifact that would protect the forest from being plowed, as a child I had learned that stones can help heal the earth as well as people.

Otherwise, what I know about the healing power of rocks I have learned from pure epiphany. This may sound crazy, but rocks—especially artifacts manufactured by our ancestors—have occasionally spoken to me and sent me pictures, sometimes even movies, when I picked them up. With the aid of a rock, I have not only seen the past but, in a sense, lived it. I have seen through the eyes of those who lived hundreds or thousands of years ago. I have felt the anguish, pain, sadness, and suffering of the person who once carried the rock, and I have even felt their deaths, at times. I have seen the turmoil of the westward movement of people being driven from their homelands, only to have to war with the people they were encroaching on in their new assigned territory. I have seen lives taken in retribution and rage. I have felt the tears of those watching their people die right before their eyes, when they had absolutely no more capability than I did to stop it.

It is a strange feeling to see through someone else's eyes and not have any control whatsoever. You are, in a sense, just an observer; you can do nothing, even when a tomahawk is planted in the middle of your chest. To tell you the truth, being able to see this way is, at times, scary as hell, but I wouldn't trade this gift for ten million dollars. I have had glimpses of village life before we messed things up, and the daily goings-on were a beautiful thing to see. The people were always much happier than the stoic Indian we have all come to know and love. Much play went on, but the play always had a life lesson, and, most of the time, the children learned without even being aware they were being taught.

Such visions are brought to me by the stones and the people who carried them long ago. In turn, the knowledge I obtain from these visions has proved to be very helpful in aiding me as a healer and as a person today. As a healer, I try to incorporate all the tools the Creator has given me, for he knows all the natural wonders of healing and I, for one, trust him.

One day, a few friends and I found ourselves indulging in a great passion of ours. My neighbor Richard, Dan "the rock man," and I headed to the pit on Highway 35, near Maiden Rock, Wisconsin, to go agate picking. Because in the past we had often been asked to leave, we decided to sneak around to the back side of the pit. This would place us a little over a half mile from the rock pile we wanted to delve through.

My friends arrived ahead of me, leaving me to walk the half mile from the cars alone. When I was about halfway there, an artifact started "calling" to me. It wanted me to come and get it. I made a 140-degree turn to my left, heading away from my friends, and started walking toward the Mississippi River.

As I walked, the rock kept calling, steering me in the right direction. Eventually, I came upon a channel that had been dug in the 1920s so that the people who owned the future gravel pit could wash the gravel. The depth of the channel was about ten feet, the width at the bottom about twelve feet, and it tapered back at forty-five degrees. I turned, walking upstream beside the channel, as the rock continued to call to me. The farther upstream I went, the narrower the channel became and the louder the rock called. In time, the channel narrowed so much that I was stepping on each side of it, uncomfortably at first. But then, farther on, it evened out to about a foot wide.

Finally, the calling became so loud that I couldn't tell where it was coming from. I continued upstream a bit more and stopped at a little white waterfall. It stood four or five inches high.

I don't know where you are, I thought.

"Look down," I heard. So I reached down into the waterfall and came up with the stone that had spoken to me.

When I picked the stone up, I saw a young native man rubbing one rock on another. It was winter, and, ever so patiently, he continued to rub the rock. The young man was about sixteen, and his folks were with him in the wigwam. This vision went on for some time.

In the next scene, I see that the young man is about eighteen and has a wife and a new baby girl. I can tell by their clothing and their large fire that it is again wintertime.

The next scene shows me that the girl is now about six years old. She has a brother about four and a baby sister who is in a cradle board. The rock is gradually taking the shape of an adze, a hide-scraping tool. It is almost ready to put the bevels on it. I notice that the man always works on it during the coldest part of the winter. The moon is that of the snapping twigs (February), and the new gray in his hair is not yet as white as the snow on the roof, but—at about the age of only twenty-six!—he is already becoming an elder in the tribe.

I see no metal utensils inside the wigwam, indicating that this is pre–Iron Age. The pots are made of birch, some with the bottoms stained black from brewing tea. The knives are flint. The plates are wooden, as are the bowls. The clothes are buckskin, and the beadwork is made from sand, drilled stone, small clams, or plain quillwork (quills flattened by women pulling them between their teeth) of various dyed colors. The clothing and the man's buffalo-hide shield have been made out of raw hide and painted in various designs.

In the next scene, I notice that the man's hair is whiter as he works on the adze. I can see that it is spring now, because no fire is burning. The man hands the stone to his daughter, who appears to be about sixteen, maybe seventeen. She takes the stone and then hands it to her grandmother for inspection.

The grandmother looks it over very slowly, very carefully. Finally, a smile emerges on her face as she says, "You are a very fortunate young woman. You will make lots of good leather with this adze, and when you are long gone and even your great-great-grandchildren are gone, this tool will live on. We will call it "Snow Blossom's tool." I name it after you, as you were born during a late snowstorm, after the blossoms were out. And when your hair starts to turn white and it is time to pass it on to your granddaughter, be sure you pass the name on, too. It is important to give a name and life to the tool; it will serve you better that way. And remember, this is *your* tool; it does not belong to whomever you marry. Now, let us walk in the woods and find a handle for it. Bring your tobacco pouch. I will teach you the prayers for this."

I see the old woman walking in the woods, looking at this tree and that. The girl asks, "Is this one right?"

"No," the grandmother answers each time.

Finally, they come upon a young white ash tree, probably only five or six years old and about three inches in diameter. The grandmother says, "This is the one. Now take a pinch of tobacco, and repeat after me."

The grandmother speaks loudly and clearly: "Oh Great Spirit, we come this day to thank you for allowing this perfect tree to grow in this perfect place so that we can make our tool. We are here to beg the tree to forgive us any injury that we may do to it, but also to give it light and life and power that it would not have had without this ceremony. Also, Creator, watch over this place and this tree so that it is not disturbed until it is time to be harvested. We love, honor, and thank you, Great Spirit, for the infinite wisdom you gave our ancestors so that we now know the things we know."

Having said the prayers, which her granddaughter dutifully repeated, the old woman shows the girl the sacred symbols to draw in the air so that the tree and the stone they will leave to grow into it will be invisible to any other people who happen by. She ties some dried sinew in a certain pattern to the tree to let her own people know to whom this tool-to-be belongs.

These ceremonial tasks completed, the grandmother takes her knife and saws the top of the tree off level, a bit over three feet from the ground, just above two opposing limbs the size of her middle finger. Except for those two limbs, she also cuts off the rest of the limbs from the ground up. She then says prayers under her breath so that only the Creator can hear them. Finally, she scrapes bark off the inner side of the two limbs, about a foot or so above where they separate from the remaining trunk.

The old woman says to her granddaughter, "Hold the stone straight up from the trunk between the limbs at three fingers distance. When that is done, the old woman wraps one limb around the stone, then the other, and pulls them together on top of it. She brings them together where the bark is missing, because at that spot the wood will graft together and the two limbs will merge, holding the stone securely.

From a little birch-bark basket, the grandmother pulls out an inch-wide strip of wet rawhide five or six feet long. Up a foot or so from the stone adze, she wraps the rawhide around the two limbs, being careful not to overlap it. She says to her granddaughter, "When you help your own granddaughter make a tool like this, be sure not to overlap the rawhide. Otherwise, it will strangle the tree." (Unlike today's plastic binds, unless rawhide is overlapped it always loosens in the humidity, allowing a tree to expand as it grows. And after a while, the birds start eating the rawhide, loosening it even further.)

The granddaughter asks, "How long do I leave the rawhide on the tree?"

The old woman replies, "It is not a tree anymore; it is a handle with limbs that will grow together to hold the stone in place. You won't have to worry about the rawhide, because the birds and creatures know just how long to leave it."

Next, I see the granddaughter, who is now a young woman with a cradle board on her back, visiting the tree. I see that about half of the rawhide has been eaten by the birds and mice for winter food. The scene that follows is again of the young woman heading back to the handle, only this time there is a different baby in the cradle board, and a girl of maybe five years of age walks with the woman.

"Your great-grandmother taught me how to make this handle for the stone that your grandfather made for me when I was a girl," the woman says.

When they arrive, the woman hangs the cradle board in a tree near the young ash tree whose limbs are being shaped. The ash is now two or three times the height it was when her grandmother found it. But since the growth of a tree is all from the top, the stone itself is only a few inches higher than it was when it was placed there.

"Where is my great-grandmother?" asks the child.

"She finished her lessons, so she went to the spirit land," answers the mother.

"Did I ever meet her?" the child asks.

"Yes," says the mother, "although you probably don't remember. But be aware that she will come to you when you need something."

"What is her name?" the child innocently asks.

"Sweetheart," the mother said, "it is not polite to speak of the dead. It is taboo, but you are young, so you can be excused. Just remember to speak of her only as your great-grandmother. Now I have to thank the Creator for keeping this handle-tree safe from those who would ruin it for making leather."

Holding up a pinch of tobacco in her right hand, the woman says, "Aho, Creator and Great Mystery. I am here to thank you for keeping this tree invisible to prying eyes, for keeping it safe. I am also here to beg the tree's forgiveness for what I am about to do and to accept its thanks for helping it to live forever by becoming a tool for the many generations that will come." (Little did she know that, in a mere five hundred to a thousand years, her way of life would disappear and her tool would be lost, not to resurface for almost another nine hundred years until the gravel-pit owner dug the channel.)

After finishing the prayer, the woman takes her flint knife from its sheath and cuts the tree trunk off three feet below the stone. Then, six inches above the stone, she cuts off the top of the tree now lying on the ground. And there it is at last—the finished adze, with its long handle topped by the shaped stone firmly embedded in wood. The woman puts the cradle board back on, takes the hand of her other child, and, carrying her new hide scraper, walks back to her village.

The woman's village is situated above the Mississippi River, in what would later be called Wisconsin, although the name by which the woman's family knows the land is *Oosconsin*. As she comes down the hill, her view encompasses the entire community of birch- and elm-bark wigwams. The large lodge, where the grand council meets to discuss tribal business or do healings, is about eighteen feet high and twenty-four feet in diameter. It is covered in birch bark.

Some distance from the central village stands the moon lodge. This is where the women go while they are on moon time (meaning their menstrual cycle). In the moon lodge, they do not cook or do any type of work at all. They are pampered for a week, working on hobbies or making female clothing or items for their own regalia.

The village is full of life. Young boys play the hoop game: One of the boys rolls a hoop ten yards in front of another group of boys. The rest shoot at it with little bows and arrows. At one of the fires, a few adult males teach some of the teenage boys how to knap flint axes, arrowheads, and knives. Women are using antlers to place hot stones into birch pots to boil the soup.

I watch as the woman with her adze makes her way to her father's wigwam, where he sits outside his lodge. He smiles at seeing the stone again. After this many years, his white hair flashes in the warm spring sunshine. The canyons around his eyes show his happiness at being able to touch the hide scraper, which now has a handle.

When the woman and her grandmother placed the stone in the ash tree so long ago, the handle-to-be would have fit her hand nicely. But her grandmother said to her, "Trees grow, so you will have to take the handle to your father to have him scrape it down to fit your hand. If we had put the stone in a smaller tree, though, the weight would have bent it like a drawn bow."

Now, seeing the stone with its thick handle, the man says to his daughter, "I will work on it, but you must come once a month so that I can see how it fits your hand."

In the next scene, I see the woman checking the fit, smiling and nodding her head in agreement. I see the father handing the hide scraper to the daughter—only now it has a soft, padded, buckskin handle on it. The woman uses the fine tool, into which so much work has gone, until she is gray, and then she passes it down to her only granddaughter.

I see that happening over and over and over again—the old women giving the hide scraper to their granddaughters. I witness this transfer maybe a hundred and fifty or two hundred times. I feel like I am sitting in an H. G. Wells time machine, where the years tick by like seconds.

Finally, time slows down. I am in the same spot, only the woods are now prairie. The only woods left are down by the river, with a few scrub trees growing around the village. It is springtime. The village is mostly sleeping, except for some posted guards. Suddenly, a couple of warriors come running in and wake everyone up. I notice that the village consists mostly of old people and children. Most of the men must have gone away on a hunting party.

After the alarm has been sounded, the women gather up their useful and sacred items. I watch them as they run away from the village. By now, twenty or so warriors are visible, gathering up war clubs, bows and arrows, and knives to make a stand. The people never left the village unguarded; these men have been out on the trails as an advanced warning system for instances exactly like this one.

A woman is late getting out of her lodge with her ten-year-old son. She is the great-grandchild to the two-hundredth generation of the original owner of the hide scraper. The boy is carrying the scraper when the people from the other tribe attack. They outnumber the village warriors by about five to one. The villagers make a good stand, but in the melee, the boy drops or hides the hide scraper in the prairie grass, where, over time, it becomes buried under the dirt, several feet deep. The place where it was dropped will someday become the gravel pit.

Some 650 years later, in the new gravel pit, the owners dug a channel to bring water from the spring to wash the gravel they were making. Eventually, the water washed away enough dirt from the bank to allow the adze stone to roll down into the channel, where it settled under the water, making the little waterfall.

I don't really know why stones and artifacts speak to me. But I do know that there will always be a lesson or an important bit of information to be learned from them. Whether the object that comes my way is a stone with energy directly to aid in healing, or an artifact that leads me to another place and time, all I can say is that the Creator works in mysterious ways.

After putting the adze stone in my bag, I headed to the rock pile where I was suppose to meet Richard and Dan. On the way I met another rock picker, this one from St. Paul. When he asked if I was finding anything, I showed him the adze and he asked if it was for sale. I said no and he offered me a thousand dollars for it. Again, I said it wasn't for sale; I wouldn't take ten grand for it. The Creator gives me these things to learn from. That adze is worth more than any agate could ever be.

Clinics for the Creator's Work

Although I always tell people that it is the Creator who is responsible for the healing, they tend to put the healer up on a pedestal. This is not where he or she belongs. I believe I now understand how that happens, though. My clients are often people who have already been treated with Western medicine. They eventually run out of options and are told that nothing more can be done for them. Then they come to me, and, in many instances, find that their illnesses—sometimes even cancer—have gone away. I am not saying that a healer doesn't play a role, but without the Creator nothing would happen.

Healing shouldn't be about money, but therein is the dilemma: in this day and age, it is a fact that it takes money to survive. Years ago, my former wife, Martha, and I ran an ad in the newspaper in an attempt to assemble a group of healers who would agree to hold a free clinic. When one couple walked in, I felt an instant dislike for the woman. And it was an *intense* dislike, which is not a typical reaction for a healer. Thinking I needed to explore this feeling, I did a past-life regression for myself. This required going into a deep meditative state, something like the process of self-hypnosis. I needed to go far enough into the past to recognize where I had encountered the woman's energy before. When I did, I discovered that this was the fifth time she and I had been in the same life as healers. She was always focused on money or wealth. My focus was on healing and helping. In four of our previous lives, she either killed me herself or had me killed. It is no wonder that at the first sight of her I had such a strong feeling of wanting to rip off her head. Not the normal reaction of a healer.

This past-life exercise not only explained my overwhelming reaction to that woman, it also caused me to reflect in general about the initial feelings we have when we meet people. There are three ways it can go: you may meet someone and instantly like them; you may instantly dislike them; or you may feel neutral about them, being open to wait and see what happens. If you like the person, you can be sure you were friends or relatives in one or more past lives, leaving no or little work to do with them. You can just be friends. If you instantly *dislike* the person, though, then there surely is work to do. In another life he or she must have hurt you in some way, either physically, emotionally, or spiritually. If the hurt was physical, you must accept the possibility that this person might have even killed you.

Regarding the woman who answered our ad, I did my fire ceremonies and eventually became friends with her in this lifetime, but I didn't turn my back to her, ever. Now I *can't* turn my back to her, because she crossed over recently. I am hoping the talks we had helped her to understand her lesson so that she can move up the spiral of the spirit land. "Bless her," I ask the Creator.

As the meeting for the free healing center progressed, most people thought it was a good idea. I figured that, with enough healers, we would each be able to donate one day a week of free service to people. Most were persuaded. However, the couple I mentioned above said they needed money to provide the service. They said they couldn't do it otherwise, so the meeting broke up and we never did get the free healing center going.

It was after this turn of events that, in 2001, I decided to open the free wellness clinic in Hayward, Wisconsin, on my own. I wanted to show that it could be done. When the clinic was up and running, we were doing ten to fifteen healings a day, even though we weren't open full time. Within two years, we were seeing fifteen to twenty people a day. In the third year, I became quite burned out and tired of the thirty-mile driving commute. That was when I moved the healing center back to the town of Spooner, where I lived. I believe donations at the Hayward clinic would have kept it going forever if I hadn't moved it.

At the Spooner location, it didn't take long to get to 50 healings a week; then the number soared to 120 in six days. From the first of January, 2010, to the fifteenth of June, 2010, my apprentices and I did 1,500 healings, and we finished the year with 3,010. On January 1, the number of healings in my appointment book was 14,404; and on December 31, the last entry number was 17,414. The reward is how good it feels at the end of the day to know that I have helped fifteen to twenty people solve or get over their problems.

One day, a woman came in who had had cancer for twelve years. Her doctor had told her that he had already provided her with all the treatments he could and that he considered her condition terminal. I asked the Creator to change her genetics from mutated to non-mutated. She had some small tumors on her chest, and, after the healing, they continued to grow (although I could see no malignancy in them). This was the first time I had seen benign tumors on the *outside* of the body. I wasn't sure what to do. I told her I would pray and see what I could find out about them.

About two weeks after I started praying, my Oneida grandmother came to me in a dream. She took me for a walk down a dirt road. One of the things she showed me was chaga—a tumor-like growth that is found on birch trees but, unlike a common mushroom, is hard rather than soft. In Oneida, chaga is called *stowachi*. As Gram said the word *stowachi* in the dream, it took me back fifty years, to the first time she had shown it to me. This time, I paid better attention to her method of how to clean the fungus and make tea from it.

The outside of the stowachi, Gram told me, can help clear up nasty skin conditions such as eczema and psoriasis. You combine equal parts of the bark of the chaga and wild grape bark. Next, you boil them in water to make a wash. Use two cups of mixed bark per gallon of water. Boil it for forty-five minutes. Then, you let it sit until it is cool; and, just before going to bed, bathe in it and let it dry on your skin naturally—do not use a towel. Then, at the crack of dawn, go to a spring hole or artesian well and wash the mixture off. Of course, you must thank the Earth Mother for her healing medicine and the Creator for making things work as they do.

As it turned out, my dream of Gram was the answer to my prayer. With the use of chaga and turkey tail, the woman's tumors shriveled up like grapes do when you make them into raisins. Then they just fell off. She told me the doctors just didn't know what to think of it! I said that it was the Creator's work and that everything he does from the largest to the smallest healing is a miracle.

I have learned from Gram that the rust-colored material on the inside of the chaga can be soaked in a gallon of lukewarm water for forty-eight hours. Then it may be refrigerated, if you want. But do not use hot water and then refrigerate the solution, because chaga is a living organism, similar to a yogurt or yeast culture. If the water is too hot, you won't benefit from it at all; you will merely kill it. I find the yuppies' craze to drink chaga with coffee funny. They pay a high price for something they are killing with boiling water. You can get the medicine from chaga only if you leave it in lukewarm water for forty-eight hours.

One benefit of the inside of the chaga is that it eats living cancer cells; it sure seems to make tumors shrink faster than chemotherapy does. In fact, I recently heard from a client who had needed a liver transplant, but because of his cancer the doctors would not do it. I treated him with some chaga "tea," and three months later he got his new results back. He is now on the transplant list because his cancer is gone.

One strong caution: Be sure to never self-treat with any herbal remedies without knowing *exactly* what you are doing. Understanding can be the difference between healing and dying, as many plants have poisonous attributes.

From Skeptic to Believer

At my office in Hayward, Wisconsin, many people come through the doors: people from every religious belief, race, and creed. Some are skeptics at heart, not eager to believe in the works of a healer. Many of my new clients have heard of me and have been curious about what I do long before they come to my center. It isn't until they have suffered for years and the doctors have given up on them that they seek me out as their last hope. On the other hand, there are people who can't wait for the opportunity to smell the burning sage and hop right up onto the table.

My clients are people who believe, people who do not believe, people who are Christian, and people who are atheists. What they all have in common is that they come from different walks of life and have different belief systems.

For example, four women who were atheistic skeptics (judging by their accents, I believe they were from Chicago) stopped by my

Hayward center. They had actually come to give me a hard time. As they entered, they were smirking about the literature and giggling at the sacred objects hanging on the wall. I sat at my desk, amused at their antics.

One woman ventured a little farther into the office and asked how I did the healing.

"Well," I said, "I use energy. Why don't you come in? There's nothing here that will hurt you." By the way she and her friends were making fun of the sacred objects, I had a feeling that they didn't believe in the Creator.

The others had been listening in. "Where do you get the energy from?" one of them asked. I told her that I channel it. She then wanted to know *exactly* where I got the energy to channel. I told her it comes from the Creator and that the Creator actually does the healing.

"I don't believe in God," the first woman said.

I replied, "That's okay." All this time, she stayed forty feet across the room from me. Soon, her friends whispered something to her and left.

"Why don't you let me do a healing on you?" I asked.

"I don't need a healing," she responded.

"What about your headache?" I challenged.

"How do you know I have a headache?" she asked.

"I can feel it clear over here," I said. I asked her how long she had had the headache. She told me about a day and a half.

"You seem like a college-educated woman," I said. I went on to say that I had about fifteen minutes between clients and was willing to fit her in. She said she had only five minutes and that I probably couldn't do anything, anyway. I repeated that she seemed well-educated and suggested that she should, at the very least, be open to the possibility that I could help her. I also said that she wouldn't know unless she tried. With that, she got up on the table and *allowed me to try*.

I worked on her for exactly five minutes. After the first minute she said, "I think my headache is getting better." After the second minute, she happily affirmed, "My headache is definitely getting better." After the third minute, she proclaimed, "My headache is almost gone." In the fourth minute, I wrapped her in a cocoon, as I do all my clients, and let her get up.

She got off the table, walked around the waiting room, and began telling the people seated there that her headache had gone away. After talking to a few of them, she realized what she was doing. Seeing the smile on my face, she asked me what my charge was.

"There is no charge, but if you like, you can make a donation," I said.

She then asked, "How do you really do that?"

I replied, "I didn't do it. I am but a simple human; the entity that you don't believe in did it."

"But I told you that I don't believe in God," she challenged.

"That's alright," I calmly replied, "because the Creator believes in *you*—as he does, in fact, all his children."

At that point, the woman dropped a check on the desk and left with one of the most puzzled expressions I have ever seen. I find it interesting that many skeptics have come to me over the years. After their healings have been successful, they still may not use the words *Creator* or *God*, but they almost all admit to believing that there is some kind of higher power out there. Another thing I have noticed is that, once you convince a skeptic, they become your biggest advocates. Since I am but a man like any other, I can truly do no healing. All you have to do is get out of the way and let the Creator do his work.

Medicine Men, Shamans, and Charlatans

Having just told a story about convincing a skeptic, I want to add that, in some cases, skepticism can be healthy and appropriate. When you are seeking a healer, beware of charlatans. Sometimes they call themselves "medicine men" and sometimes "shamans," but, by whatever name, a charlatan is not practicing healing to serve the client and the Creator. He is practicing a trade to serve himself.

When Europe was tribal, the visionaries of the tribes were called *shamans. Shaman* is a word for "healer" that comes from between Germany and Yugoslavia. It migrated to South America when the Nazis fled there at the end of World War II. Meeting medicine men in South American countries, the Nazis called them by the word they knew: *shaman*. But please don't call medicine men shamans, as most medicine men I know take offense. For me, it works either way, as I have German in my background, although I associate more with the term *medicine man* because of my training.

And regardless of what you call someone, be sure to check their reputation before going to him or her for healing. I think that some people say they have trained with medicine men in South America because no one has any way to check on the truth. Suspicious, eh? We all know what happens when untrained people try to use our traditional medicine techniques: people die!

The sweat lodge is a method of healing that originated in North— not South—America. (Why would people go out of their way to sweat in South America when you can sweat there just lying in the shade?)

People, please be careful whom you trust as far as ceremony goes, as it can be dangerous. I love you and don't want you to die. Real trainers teach never to use things for the sweat lodge that give off poisonous gas when they are heated—like polypropylene, for instance. Also, never, ever burn wood inside the lodge, as the wood makes carbon monoxide and carbon dioxide. Burning wood inside a lodge can be a death sentence. I heard of one white guy with no training who decided to do a sweat by himself and found used rocks in the lodge rock pit. Assuming the rocks had been heated inside the lodge, he almost killed himself trying to do it that way. I say this is for those of you who want to build your own lodge, which I don't recommend. Don't run off half-cocked and get hurt. Get some training!

A true medicine man would never have people fast before a sweat-lodge ceremony and then feed them just before they go in, as this can cause cramping and many other repercussions, as well. This is another adulteration of our indigenous ways that I hear has occurred. It seems that people like to take our practices and run with them before they truly study them. But by training with a medicine man, they could find deeper meaning in the ceremonies and learn to do them in the correct way.

I don't think there is anything accidental about the way a certain lodge was conducted in Sedona, where an unstudied person charged people ten thousand dollars each to attend a seminar that included a sweat lodge. Some of the participants died because the leader used polypropylene in the lodge. I think that action was criminal. You must never use our medicine for profit, or I can guarantee that you will slip many levels down the spiritual spiral of life. Do you really want to come back with a many-times-worse life than you have had in this one? Granted, these are just my thoughts, but they are the thoughts of a trained medicine man who earned the right actually to run a lodge by doing the work, going on vision quest, and studying for years with trained medicine men.

And you who are charging a thousand dollars apiece to people who want to go on a quest: You are not doing the right thing in sending them out without protection. I say to you, see a real medicine person and learn before another Sedona happens! Stop before you have to start at the bottom and end up living in a cardboard box in your next life. I really feel sad about the journey you are on. Charging people to go to South America to study can only bring you down levels in your next life. Why don't you promote studying with medicine men or women in the north? Because there is no profit margin in it? If you wanted truly to help people, you would find a way to do it without scamming them.

Balance and the Medicine Wheel

I recall walking down one of the dirt roads near Big McKenzie Lake with my grandmother. It was springtime, and the fiddleheads were up in the forest.

"What are those?" asked Gram.

"Ferns," I replied.

Gram corrected me. "They are brackens. They are edible but poisonous, unless you boil them twice and change the water before the second boiling. They taste like asparagus, and they're good. There are lots of things to eat in the woods, but you have to know how to treat them."

"Like what?" I asked.

"Oh, many things," she said. "Did you see the cattails growing in the swamp across from the lake?"

"Yes."

"In a couple of weeks, when they turn yellow, we will boil some and see what they taste like."

"What *do* they taste like?"

Gram replied, "You'll just have to wait and see."

Later, when we finally did cook some up, I found that they tasted like corn on the cob. Gram taught me that, among the cattail's many gifts to the people, its roots can be pounded and used as a poultice for burns and sores. Also, the young flower heads can be made into a tea to cure dysentery.

"Everything is perfect as it is," Gram said. "There is no disease that the Creator did not make a cure for. Everything is in his exact balance: There is disease. There is also a cure. There is no sadness without happiness, and no happiness without a little sadness. If you were not sad sometimes, how would you know when you were happy? Or, if you didn't know happiness, how would you know when you were sad? It is like pain. There is only so much pain in the world. Hold out both of your hands."

When I did, Gram said, "All of your fingers represent all the people on this earth." She pointed to the tip of my little finger. "The whole human race carries only enough pain for the tip of that finger," Gram said, using a metaphor a five-year-old could understand. "And pain is a great teacher. So it is our responsibility as healers to learn our lessons so that we can let our own pain go. The Creator then will send that pain to someone else so that they can learn *their* lessons. It is all a matter of balance."

Sometimes the Creator's balance can take a long time to come about. Early in my life, I didn't want to be a healer. But now I am doing between fifty and one hundred healings per week and grateful for it. I find that most people's problems come from their heart boxes. Some problems, like arrhythmia, come from a genetic source but are easily corrected. I fixed my own wife's arrhythmia about nine years ago, and she hasn't had a skipped beat since.

My wife's arrhythmia may have been related to a tendency to panic, inherited from past lives, that could definitely throw her off balance. She had an unreasonable fear of spiders—and, sure enough, when she worked on it, she found that the reason stemmed from something in her heart box. It seems that, many lifetimes ago, before the Europeans came, she was a native man. While hunting in the jungles of what would later be called Colombia, the man went hunting one morning and hit a howler monkey with his bow and arrow. He kept his eyes skyward as he followed the path of the monkey through the canopy. He was trying so hard to keep up with the howler that he didn't notice the monkey had left the man's tribal territory; soon he was well into the neighbors' territory before he realized it. By that time, it was too late: the neighboring tribe captured him for trespassing.

They staked the man out, sprawled on the jungle floor, for the jaguar deity. In essence, he was to be lunch. But before the jaguar got to him, a bird-eating spider bit him in the neck, leaving him paralyzed. The spider was eating his face while he screamed, helpless to fight against the ropes that bound him. Not that there was any pain; it was just the sound of the spider eating his flesh that bothered him.

It is no wonder, then, that my wife had such a phobia against spiders. Can you imagine the terror of being staked there, watching a furry spider the size of a dinner plate chomp on your face—and feeling it, too, until the venom kicked in and made everything numb—knowing there was nowhere you could go?

I have found that we carry past-life issues from life to life until we learn our lessons from them. My wife did a fire ceremony to forgive the situation with the spider. Now, instead of running from spiders, she catches them in a glass most of the time. But if you are a spider, you don't want to surprise her, since she is definitely prone to action.

I have no problem understanding how one can develop a fear of something such as spiders from past lives. But I do have a hard time understanding how one can continue to live holding onto these fears. Like Gram always said, you must walk in love, not fear. Otherwise, your responses to many things—major issues as well as tiny spiders— can be out of balance and unhealthy for your spirit.

In the native tradition, a profound image for perfect balance is the medicine wheel. The wheel is not about specific herbs and medicines. Instead, it is a rich system of symbols and associations used to help bring about answers on a spiritual plane. It has four parts, just as nature has four seasons and the pattern of four shows up in nature over and over again in, for example, roots, trunks, limbs, and leaves. Each part on the wheel is associated with a season of the earth and with one of the four cardinal directions. It also represents one of the four stages of human life.

East on the wheel is the season of spring. Just as it is the time of renewal for the earth, it is the direction of our infancy, when we are new on the planet.

South on the wheel represents summer, the time of fast growth for plants and animals and the time of our adolescence, when we begin growing up and learning in leaps and bounds.

West on the wheel is autumn: the time of full maturity for the harvesting of crops and the time of our adulthood, when we raise our own families and start to obtain wisdom.

North on the wheel represents winter, the time of snow when the plants and animals are resting. This is the season of life of eldership, when our wisdom comes into its own and we become the teachers.

If we live long enough, we may lose our teeth, become incontinent, and head back to infancy, thus completing the circle. From the spirit land we come, and to the spirit land we go. And all animals are just like people in this pattern, only on a different schedule.

I have found that most native nations have a medicine wheel with colors of some sort. Just as medicine wheels may differ from one culture to another, so may each color on them.

In my Oneida way and belief, the color red signifies the east. That is our spiritual direction. For example, if you are outside doing prayers at the crack of dawn, you will notice that, just before the sun comes up, the sky turns red. Sometimes this happens ever so briefly, sometimes for a longer period. If you listen at this time, the Creator will give you the answers you seek, as long as you are using tobacco as instructed by him.

Yellow signifies the south, the direction of the heat that jumpstarts the spring, so that things can grow and prosper again. This is where the Standing People (the trees) live, who slow the wind down so that it will be tolerable and not dry things out too much. Just as the south is about hot summer days—when the sun is high and glows bright yellow and everything is growing like crazy—it is also about expansion of the physical, the emotional, the mental, and the spiritual in human life.

Black signifies the west. This is the direction of the Thunder Beings, the Waniggi who have the power to bring the blood of the Earth Mother to her in the form of life-sustaining water and the power to take away with lightning, which can destroy a life.

Finally, the color white signifies the north. This is the place where the courage of my people originates: the courage to face the difficulties in life and to speak our truths, to carry on as we always have in spite of the assimilation, death, and disease. It is the courage to keep our way of life through all adversity.

Each direction on the medicine wheel is also associated with spirit animals that help bring the answers to questions about healing. The animal that brings messages from the north is the snowy owl. In the *far* north, it is the white bear. Look to the red fox, the badger, and the black bear for messages from the east. Look to the otter, the deer, and the cougar for messages from the south, and, from the west, the spotted or golden eagle and the grizzly bear.

These are the things I have been taught. They are the ways of my medicine; I cannot speak for others.

Here is a story Gram told about the wind and the need for balance: A long, long time back, when the Creator's first children were on the planet, the Creator gave the earth the Four Grandfathers, one for each of the cardinal directions.

To the Grandfather of the North, for instance, the Creator said, "Your color will be white, the color of winter. You shall watch over the great white bear and the snowy owl. You will bring courage to the people so that they may face the trials that will come, and you will be in charge of the cold. . . . " And so on. To each grandfather he assigned a season, a color, a stage and aspect of life, and animals, just in the pattern I have described above.

To the Grandfathers of the East and West, the Creator also assigned winds: The Grandfather of the East—the direction of spiritual matters—was in charge of the east winds that blow across the earth, and the Grandfather of the West was in charge of the winds that come from that direction, bringing the sacred rain that nourishes every living thing and the warm breezes that keep the tiny winged ones away.

When the Creator was finished with all four assignments, he said, "So, does everyone understand his job?"

"Well, which one of them is the most important?" asked Grandfather of the East.

"No one is more so than another. You are all here to help my children," answered the Creator.

But one day, Grandfather of the East decided that he was going to make the morning wind, but Grandfather of the West said, "The Earth Mother thirsts, so let me bring the rain."

"No!" puffed Grandfather of the East. "It is I who am blowing today."

Thus started the struggle between the two Grandfathers—East always wanting to blow west and West always wanting to blow east, West always wanting to bring rain and East always trying to bring his own storms.

And so it is. The struggle between the two winds continues to this day. In the same way, people in one place struggle with people in other places, never seeking—it seems—to get along, but always striving for one-upmanship, trying to be better than their neighbors. The standoff that divides our politics gets ever more intense, and it is the ordinary person who gets blown about in the crosswind.

Balance at Work

I remember Gram saying, "Watch the signs for the polar shift I have been telling you about, and when you start seeing them, prepare. Put stuff away to help you survive." (She was talking about the end of the Mayan calendar in 2012, which came and went without any dramatic change, but we can never be sure when the shift will happen. I hope we can raise the vibrational level high enough to stop it, but the poles could conceivably change at any time.)

"What about you?" I asked as a child.

"I have taught you that the earth's magnetic poles have changed three times before, and it is said they are weakening in preparation of doing it again. But it won't happen until long after I'm gone. I would have to be 150 years old to see it, although I might be back by then. But I think I am going to sit this one out. I think, after this present life, I'll have some say in my coming back next time," she said.

"What do you mean, you'll have some say?"

"We come back into new lives to learn lessons that we still need, and I think I'm getting to the point when I'm finished. As I have taught you, the spirit land is in a spiral that moves ever up and sunwise (clockwise), and our job is to get to *attainment* so that we can sit at the feet of the Creator and the master healer that folks call Jesus."

"Why do you call him a master healer?" I asked.

"Who does the healing?" she asked.

"The Creator," I said proudly.

"That's right. Even the healer Jesus healed through the Creator. Like you and me, he was a vessel to transmit the Creator's love, and the Creator's love is where healing comes from. And if you transmit love, guess what comes back?"

"More love," I said.

"That's exactly right," she exclaimed. "You are definitely getting it."

I was doing well—two for two!

"Jesus had the ability to transmit love and also get the people to do it. So if you get your clients to transmit love, their healings will go much faster," Gram went on.

"And the same is true for the healer; for, as you transmit love to the client, love also comes back to you with a healing benefit. So, you see, the effect is twofold. It would do no good if the very people who were trying to do the Creator's work became burned out, now, would it? The Creator, in his infinite wisdom, made it to work this mutual way. Healing going only toward the client wouldn't make any sense, because the healers doing the Creator's work would get used up faster than they could help people.

"And remember, the Creator is not judgmental, jealous, or angry. Those ideas are just spread to make money for organizations that tell you they can save your soul . . . it's all bull! All you have to do is love the Creator—or not. Free will is a great thing."

Gram continued, "You will have clients who come to you and expect you to save them, so it's your job to tell them that only two beings can save them: the Creator and they themselves. You will have people begging you to save their lives, but unless they are willing to do their part and completely trust in the Creator, the healing won't go as well. They will say, 'I hope he can help me,' or 'I believe he can help me,' or 'I hope he will find me worthy.' That's not what I mean. They need to say, 'I know he can help me' and 'I deserve it.' If they don't come to you trusting the Creator, it's up to you to let them know that this is what they need to do.

"Even then, some people will say one thing when they are at your healing place and do something completely different when they are in their homes. If you can't get them on the right track, it may be because they are not supposed to get on the right track. It's their choice and God's choice. Because the Creator gave us free will to do or not do as we choose, there is no forcing by him or by anyone who does his work. We can't do healing unless we have a total commitment from the client who comes willingly to us.

"You will have people ask you to do long-distance healing on someone without their knowledge, but we can't. That's working on the gray side, which we don't do. Always stay in the light, never move to the gray or dark side."

So, as Gram taught, it is imperative that we have people's permission when we do healing work on them; they must know full well what is going on. In the rare circumstances when a client doesn't have the ability to speak, we need to get permission from mom, dad, or someone close to the person, and then we must also obtain permission from the person's spirit.

In addition to invoking the Creator, I now use "projecting to the universe" as an aid in healing and in my own personal life. If you project or ask for something, you have 95 percent more chance of getting it than if you don't. Once you send out to the universe what you truly want, it will come back to you—as Gram once told me—amplified and magnified. But you must sincerely believe that it will. (When I first wrote this sentence, I thought it was true. Now I'm not so sure, as all my atheist clients who don't believe in God get healed, too. But they *know* the healing will work, even though they don't believe in God.)

I use such projection every time I do a healing, knowing that all things are possible through the Creator. Even when people don't believe in him, the Creator still heals them because he truly believes in all his children, and he gives us free will to believe or not believe as we choose. Therefore, contrary to popular belief, he doesn't judge us for whatever we do.

A simplified example of this type of faith is illustrated by a three-and-a-half-year-old boy whose mother brought him to a healing session. Upon finishing, I asked him if he would like a piece of cake or a bowl of ice cream.

"I want both," the boy firmly stated.

I happily gave him both, for he gave me a very good lesson in return. The lesson is that you *really can* have it all. You can have good health and happiness, and you can have wealth and friends. You just need to believe it in your heart and know that the Creator will deliver. It is as simple as that.

I know the Creator provides, so I never have to worry about whether I'm going to be able to pay the bills or get done what I need to do. My grandmother told me all these things when I was young. But at the time, I couldn't put it all together. I now understand about loving myself and taking care of myself. Most important, you must believe in yourself. You must believe that you are worthy of good things. Following the Red Road helps to make this possible, and knowing that the Creator can do anything makes *all* things possible—unless you would ask him to break his own laws.

I believe this is the secret to the thousands of successful healings that the Creator has done through me. I know of no healer, no matter where they are, who can do healing on their own. No matter what type or modality of healing you do, there is only one source of the power to heal. I truly know the Creator will heal my clients; I myself am no more than a channel for him. And for this opportunity to assist God the Creator, I am forever grateful.

I say again: everyone has the right to believe as they choose, and not every belief works for everybody. If I didn't speak my truth on this matter, my gram's teachings would have been for naught and I would have let her down. I might as well not have studied with her for the twenty-eight years that I did.

You can call the divine force *Creator, God, Jehovah, Allah, Wakan Tanka, Gitchi Manitou, Yahweh,* or, for that matter, the *universe.* They are just words for the same thing. The point is not, "My god is bigger than yours!" The point is having the faith to believe, or—even more than that—to know.

Many Ways to God

Once I was trying to draw a piece of glass out of the knee of a client named Bonnie. We were talking about this and that, and Bonnie said, "You ever notice how certain people tell you there is only one way to get to God?"

"Yes, but I use the example of a globe of the earth. It's like this: The globe has a multitude of grid lines running east and west and others running north and south. If you follow any of the vertical lines, where do they end up?"

"At the top of the globe, right?"

"Right—the same place as any other line on the globe. Now, it's the same with Spirit. Say that each line represents a different religion or way of believing. Again, no matter what—no matter how far apart those lines might appear to be at some points—eventually we all end up at the same place. Some people like to imagine that their line is the only line going to the ultimate destination: spirit land, or, if you wish, heaven. But sorry, people; wake up! All the lines go to the same place," I said.

"That is a good way of looking at it," said Bonnie, "and on a much bigger scale than what I usually tell people. I say that we are in Spooner, and we are going to Minneapolis. There are many routes to Minneapolis, and yours is only one way. They say no, ours is the only way. Give us some money, and we will drive you there. You won't have to do anything; you can just sit and ride."

"You are sure right about the evangelists! And they have no trouble finding people who don't want to do their work. I see it in healing every once in a while. Some people want the Creator to do everything for them, not realizing that they have to meet the Creator halfway."

"Yep, it's the same thing. I tell them I'm going to take an alternative route so I can stop here and there to do whatever work I need to do, and even with the stops, I will probably beat them to Minneapolis," said Bonnie.

"Right. It is up to each of us to do the things we need to do to reach the ultimate goal: the trip to the spirit land, so that we can move up. It's all so simple." I finished the healing, and Bonnie said that she was now armed with even more arguments for the narrow-minded people she meets.

One important way to move up on the spiral of life is forgiveness. A big part of my healing work is getting people to forgive—themselves and others. I have heard people say, "There is no way I can forgive him" (or her). I ask, so how does that help anything? If we hold hurt and pain in our heart boxes, who does it hurt? Surely not the people we are angry at! They could care less. Do they get an ulcer? Not a chance. They are off being happy while you are wallowing in your own mire. So what do we do about it? The hardest thing for people to see is you being happy, especially if they are enjoying your misery. Laugh in their faces! Forgiveness is not about them. It is about you. You really don't have to like them; you are forgiving them for your own benefit. It is so simple not to get caught up in their battle on their terms. You need to control the situation with love; sending your opponent love is the last thing anyone would expect in a conflict. For the most part, it catches them completely off-guard. Now I will be like Gram and repeat myself until I am sure you have got it: Remember, you are forgiving them for whom? That's right— yourself! And you really don't have to like them, but stay at the high level where you should be; don't be drawn down. Anyone can sink to whatever level they want, but that behavior is not for anyone on the spiritual path.

Walking the Red Road

In Native American teachings, the Red Road is a concept of the right path of life. To walk the Red Road is to walk in a way that honors all creation. All of the Creator's creatures have as much right to belong in the circle of life as we do. From the tiniest tick to the largest mammal, everything is important. We should walk in such a way that not only our children, but also seven generations of grandchildren, will have it better than we do.

Anything we harm—no matter how small it may be—affects the whole web of life. When we cause the extinction of a life form, we know not what the repercussions will be, because we never live long enough to find out. The final effect of something that happened generations ago may just be rearing its ugly head, and we who are alive now wonder why: where did that come from?

Say we make the tiniest creature disappear; say that tiny creature ate the Lyme bacteria and kept it under control. Currently in many parts of the United States we are having an epidemic of Lyme disease and can't figure out the cause, when, in fact, the cause may have originated in the 1900s. Nothing in the web of life can leave it without some kind of repercussion.

I remember, as a child, my grandma and I walking to a place where we harvested ginseng. Once we got there, we saw that it was all gone. I felt heartsick over it.

Gram said in disbelief, "It is okay. Some people just don't know what is right. I have harvested here for forty years, and there have always been plenty of plants. I have never been greedy about it, but greediness is the nature of younger brothers who came across the ocean."

Can you feel how she must have felt in seeing the ginseng all gone? To me, it was devastating, until she explained about ignorance.

"I have tried to teach people that there is abundance," Gram continued, "but they live in fear—fear of lacking that very abundance. So they feel they must take as much as they can get *right now*. They do not care about tomorrow even enough, in fact, to protect their own children."

"What will be left for them?" I asked.

"In the Iroquois way, when we make decisions, we consider not only our grandchildren but also the seven generations to come. We burden ourselves with this responsibility for descendants who won't even know who we were—but that doesn't matter, as it is one of the responsibilities the Creator has charged us with. You are Oneida, so you must remember this: you need to think about your seventh-generation descendant before you do something. If everyone did so, there would be no problems with the Earth Mother. Abundance exists; it's just that most people aren't aware of it. Do you understand?" she asked.

"Yes, I think so," I replied. "If we don't take everything, if we just take what we need, there will always be enough. Right?"

"Yes, Honey, that's right. Of course, there's more to it. When you have abundance, you look at things differently. What do you suppose that difference is?"

228

"Well, if you have abundance, you have enough?"

"Remember what I said about there being two sides to everything? It is a matter of perspective. Most people look at the downside. On the upside of our present situation, I have other places to harvest ginseng. We have a wonderful day, and we will have a great harvest. We are breathing, and the Creator has blessed us with all we have. The air is clean, and we have our health. What do you think?" she asked.

"Yeah," I answered, "I think we are lucky."

"What do you mean, 'lucky'?"

"You know, Gram; we have all we need."

"How right you are, my boy, how right you are!" Gram said proudly.

She further explained, "There are challenges today that make it more difficult to stay on this path of the Red Road: greater numbers of people are living side by side with competing interests; and white, mainstream culture emphasizes money and material goods over living in harmony with the Earth Mother. Nevertheless, all things are perfect in the Creator's way. So we follow our teachings and traditions as best we can to further the advancement of all the Creator's children. Remember, if we are not part of the solution, then we are part of the problem."

I often find myself torn between the red world and the white world. It is good to remember that making the right choices about our bodies is only the half of it. We must also respect the Earth Mother. In the red world of my grandmother, we hurt the Earth Mother when we dug and blasted her. But unfortunately, to survive in the white world takes money—which sometimes involves "digging" and "blasting." To come to grips with this conflict within myself, I feel I need to join in and make sure projects are carried out in a good, respectful way. Otherwise, if I turn away and let things happen as they will, I betray my conscience. I believe the thing to do is to help by teaching respect for Mother Earth as we go.

Walking the Red Road helps keep us on the right track. Whether the issue is about Mother Earth or our own bodies, you will often find yourself faced with difficult decisions. If I hadn't followed the Red Road while I was in 'Nam, who knows where I might have ended up? I could have easily found myself doing the same as some of my white and black brothers did there, turning to whatever drugs or alcohol I could have gotten my hands on. It isn't that I didn't try pot. It's just that being on the Red Road made it easier—much easier—to stay away from it. Remembering how I was raised and doing prayers with other native soldiers also helped. In Vietnam, I held up my tobacco to the Creator along with a Modoc guy (I think) and an Apache fellow from Arizona. It felt right, and it helped me to realize that I was going to make it, as God showed me from time to time.

If I had known what the Vietnam War was going to be like, ten million dollars would not have convinced me to go through it. On the other hand, ten million dollars wouldn't be enough for me to exchange the wisdom I gained by having done so. Being on the Red Road can turn even horrific experiences into lessons. Because of it, the traumas I suffered in Vietnam have helped me in my healings, and I have been able to help a lot of veterans and nonveteran sufferers of PTSD.

I find it disconcerting that corporations are now using the Iroquois creed to rip people off—saying that we have to think of the seventh generation after us—and, at the same time, charging more for recycled paper than it costs for new. The corporations say the higher charge is to cover the cost of the additional energy needed to rework the old paper. But if it really takes more energy to make recycled paper than it does to make new paper from trees, then it can't be helping the earth. What's more, if the recycling corporations are in fact using *more* energy, not less, then they are also ripping people off by getting illegitimate tax breaks for being "green" companies. If you don't like what corporations are doing—if they are polluting the Earth Mother—let them know what you think and stop buying from them.

We are the ones in control, and we have the ability to hit the corporations where it hurts: in their bank accounts. It will take all of us working together, but we can do it. People, this is America, founded on freedom and free will: just stop buying from irresponsible companies. We have the right and the power. Take it back.

It is the same regarding politicians. Thomas Jefferson designed the United States government based on the Iroquois confederacy; but one of the things he left out was that, if a person didn't do his job, the Iroquois didn't wait for two or four years to do something about it. Our people would call a vote that very day and oust the man right then and there. To be relieved of office was extremely shameful. You could be shunned, or all manner of other ramifications could happen. So everyone worked hard to do their jobs as well as they could. If they said they were going to do something, they simply did it. There was no saying you would do something and then *not* doing it, because the people had the power to throw you out—as we have now, if we would use it!

Passing the Lessons On

A client of mine once commented on how interesting it was to hear about the ancient past. I told him that, in our way, the past is not so ancient; it is here and now. I said I was glad that my grandmother, my great-grandmother, and my father had never been placed in a white boarding school. Otherwise, their native culture would have been stripped from them. If that had happened, they couldn't have taught me the traditions of my people. As it is, I am able to record this knowledge and pass it down to my children and others. These things won't be lost to posterity. When I think about it, I realize how much knowledge has already been lost—most of it after thousands of years of use. At one time, our medicine men were so wise that smallpox, mumps, and cancer were virtually extinct in this country. That was until the Europeans reintroduced them. Most of the common diseases that we live with today originally disappeared eons ago.

The Ho-Chunk nation in Black River Falls, Wisconsin, recently asked if I could do some medicine work there. I said I was already working with the St. Croix people and some of the Lac Courte Oreilles (LCO) Ojibwa, but I could get to the Ho-Chunks maybe once a month or so. Both of their medicine men had died, and those healers had found no apprentices, so their medicine is now extinct, as far as I know. I find this most sad and am glad that I have had several apprentices. Right now, I have three apprentices with whom I am still teaching and working.

An elderly lady, seventy-five years young, once asked if she could apprentice with me, but she was shocked to hear that I have my apprentices for four years each.

"You mean I can't get a certificate in a few weeks or months?" she complained.

Sorry, no. How people can learn healing in a few months is beyond me. Think about it: Would you want the person building your house to be someone who had gone to school for three months, or would you want a master carpenter with a four-year degree who had worked in the industry for thirty years? I studied with Gram for twenty-eight years. Wisdom is seldom gained overnight. No easy fixes—it comes at a cost of years of study.

The lessons I learned from Gram have almost always pulled me through tough times. Now that I "have" them, I try to pass them on, and they often help me teach my apprentices as they go on their own journeys. One apprentice said she noticed that the more she learns, the more she sees there is to learn. Now, three months after she began her apprenticeship, she finds she's not in the same place she started from. Things that used to be important to her now mean nothing. She also says, though, that when her old friends try to pull her back into her old ruts, she still has to watch it, because it is easy to slip into other people's reality. It is good to know that she is paying attention to what I say, and what I say I got from my gram.

When I told one of my young apprentices that I loved everyone, he asked, "What about people who are just plain bad?"

"It's not our place to judge," I replied. "If I meet someone who is in a bad state, I just see someone who is wounded and needs help—as you should, too. Know that we can't walk anyone else's journey. We can only walk our own."

We can, however, walk in unconditional love. That is a way of being in which, if we see someone who is in need of aid, we try the best we can, in a gentle, loving way, to help them.

Over the years, my experience has been that if you criticize someone too bluntly, that person will just resist what you are saying. It is a natural response when things are approached in a negative way. In the Lakota tradition are the Heyokas—sacred clowns who speak and teach in a backward or negative way, saying the opposite of what they mean. For instance, if a Heyoka were to come up to you and say, "You are a disgusting individual," that would mean he likes you. But not all people can learn through such a style; we often don't understand that what seems to be negative criticism is actually meant to have a positive effect. Instead, when confronted, we dig our heels in and become even more entrenched in whatever we need to be getting away from. Learning to accept criticism is not easy to do. It is much easier for most of us, including me, to talk the talk than to walk the walk. I forgive myself in fire ceremony a lot for this human trait. But it is the way the Creator made me, and if he doesn't mind, who am I to second-guess him?

I remember Gram saying, "As a healer, you are going to have a better connection to the Creator. We need to hold ourselves to a higher standard than most, but always remember that we are human, too. Remember to take care of yourself. You can't help anyone if you are not in good shape yourself."

So every once in a while—when I do too much healing work and it starts getting to me—I remember Gram's words and take some time off for rejuvenation. I usually go to Ontario, as she once suggested, where there's no phone service, or to Iowa to pick rock. I find picking rock very satisfying. It reminds me of walking down the roads that used to be dirt, west of Trego, Wisconsin, where I was born. And there is something about communing with nature that is deeply gratifying. I don't know if it is because of my native heritage or if it is just who I am as a person. But, through my teachings, I do know that I am—as we all are—part of the Creator's plan. We are all part of the circle, as Gram said, "No more, no less."

One of Gram's most important lessons to pass on is the need to care for Mother Earth. When people used to take care of the Earth Mother, the atmosphere worked one way. Now that human beings have damaged it, it works another way. Both the atmosphere and the Earth Mother are creations of the Creator. Because he gave us free will, he won't interfere with what we do, so the atmosphere naturally reacts one way undamaged and another way damaged. But both ways are perfect as the Creator made them and are exactly right for each situation. We will learn the consequences of our actions, for good or ill.

It is common knowledge that our damage to the atmosphere is letting stuff get to us from the sun that otherwise wouldn't. Whether something is also getting to us from outer space, I'm not sure. But I do know that a lot of people are noticing the effect now. For one thing, it is easier to get tired. Even my young clients are noticing it—people who are twenty to twenty-five years old. When I was that age, I could shovel concrete all day.

In Ontario, I heard that US government scientists are doing tests on subatomic particles known as *neutrinos* under the US desert, two miles deep. Most neutrinos come from the sun. They are electrically neutral and so are not affected by electromagnetism; they can go through normal matter without stopping. The tests show that these little particles coming through the atmosphere penetrate the scientists' test plates at near the speed of light and keep right on going until they emerge on the other side of the earth. It is surprising what you can learn in Canada that you won't hear in our own country.

I often wonder about the nature of those particles. Whatever they are, they must be infinitesimally small to pass through solid rock. Before we damaged the atmosphere these particles didn't get to us, so they must have been stopped somehow. One thing I have noticed— after having worked in healing for forty-plus years and talking with thousands of clients—is that there appears to be a link between the increasing number of the neutrinos entering our atmosphere and the increasing number of people needing healings each year. This is one of the reasons I am trying to teach more apprentices: they will definitely be needed in the near future. Things are getting no better for anyone, and within a few years we will be experiencing conditions like no one has since before the last cleanse, when the poles reversed and the water washed the earth clean in Noah's day.

The economy will eventually fall apart here, just as it is doing in Russia. Prices will soar, especially those for gas and food. Growing food will become increasingly harder, as more and more ground becomes contaminated by jet-fuel hydrocarbons and dries out as the air warms up. I predict this happening within the next ten years, and all because we don't have enough sense to take care of the Earth Mother.

It seems Gram was right that I would be teaching what I have learned. I never imagined teaching, but now I do it almost unconsciously. Teaching my gram's lessons seems natural and effortless; they just seem to flow out on their own, and I find myself teaching every day during my healing work now. I am not very organized at it, but I guess that is how I was taught—in bits and pieces, as Gram saw fit. I never knew what great adventure the day would bring, and I think that is why I found life with her so exciting. I feel similar when one of my apprentices figures something out—when I drop small hints and they really get it on their own.

Like Gram, I try to keep the lessons new and simple, although, also like her, I tend to go over the same thing in a few different ways. I find it rewarding when I see a bumper sticker on a car or truck of something I've been telling people for thirty years. My cousin Denny and his wife, Betty, stopped at my place the other day after a day trip they had taken to Stillwater, Wisconsin. He'd seen a bumper sticker, handmade, in the back window of a pickup that said, "It is what it is," and he said to Betty, "I'll bet that guy knows Russell!" They both were laughing at my kitchen table with my wife, Shelly, and me. I said I wouldn't doubt that I knew the guy, or at least had seen him, as I have spoken at the Big Woods, Big Plains gathering three or four times and did the opening pipe ceremony there once or twice. So it spreads.

And speaking of spreading: one of my sisters-in-law went to a wedding in Iowa last spring where they did my fire ceremony—even though I didn't know a soul there! It was a beautiful, outdoor ceremony with a bonfire, and they changed the ceremony by offering well-wishes for the wedding couple. One of my clients must have known the couple and taught them about the fire ceremony; how perfect is that!

Healing is not always easy, but it is definitely worth it in the long run. As we ourselves become more healed, the more we want healing for everyone, as we should do. If everyone were on a healing journey—or better yet, already healed—prejudice and strife would no longer exist. I see a day coming when we will be one with each other and with the world. Maybe not tomorrow, but the time is coming, and to sense that is without a doubt a good feeling. If we all do our little part, we can accomplish this goal, and I know the Creator is pleased as I write this. So, as my gram told me, walk impeccably, and soon others will notice your smile and the way you feel about yourself. That way of being rubs off, so make sure that on your journey you rub elbows with as many people as you can.

Thinking about the clients I have had these many years, I tell my apprentices that there are things you learn from each healing. A person may come for one thing that seems very obvious, but, before you are done, something completely different shows up—some lesson about spirituality or their masculinity or femininity, for instance. It's funny that what we think we are healing is often only the precursor to why the client is really there. In some cases, even the client doesn't know the underlying issue, but with a little work on the healer's part, it can usually be brought out. This—and not just the energy work—

is actually one of a healer's main jobs, although some don't want or are afraid of the challenge.

Just being impeccable in our word isn't always enough. We need to be impeccable in our actions, thoughts, and prayers as well, always making sure that our thoughts are for everyone's highest good. I saw actions in Vietnam that served this principle, where a man gave up his life to save many of his friends. This is true impeccability. Such a man could have saved himself and let many perish, but he acted in the highest good of all.

I have been thinking for a long time about our way of healing being called "alternative medicine." That's like a modern association suddenly copying the Mona Lisa and calling theirs the "original" and the actual work an "alternative" painting, even though Leonardo da Vinci's painting has been around for hundreds of years. Similarly, just because conventional medicine now considers itself the original, how could anyone call methods that have been around for thirty or forty thousand years longer the "alternative"?

To discount what tribal people all over the world have done for healing is a shame. The medical profession will argue that our ways are not scientific, but just because our methods weren't tested in a laboratory doesn't mean they weren't put to the test millions of times. They wouldn't have lasted all those thousands of years if they hadn't worked! If you need to know the medicine, you have to learn it the way I did and not in a classroom. My grandmother made me repeat things so many times that it would be impossible to forget them. Every question I asked she answered with two questions back, with the result that I ended up answering my own questions. This is not a bad way to learn, and I use it in the training of my apprentices.

So again, to call the medicine of this land's original people "alternative" is silly. People should look at the facts! Ours is the original medicine work.

The heart of this medicine work as I know it is the Oneida fire ceremony. Reread that section to make sure you have it. If you use the ceremony, it will help you, as it has worked for me and more than forty thousand clients. By now, there are people using it who learned it from people I taught it to. It is very rewarding to pass something on and see it become greater on its own than it could be with you alone.

In Gratitude

As Gram said when I was a child, "Remember always: life is what it is. If you truly understand that, things won't seem so personal, and your time on the Earth Mother will be easier. Also, your life will be easier if you don't get into the habit of worrying. When you are older, your life will be more complicated than it is now, and people will be stressed. They will worry. Don't get caught in that trap."

What causes pain? What causes us to feel stress? Simply put, it is the sense of lack of abundance—and that is one of the biggest lessons we would do well to learn. It doesn't matter if the lack we feel is of time, money, or anything else. When we get into that state, it usually means that we are forgetting to feel gratitude. We tend to forget and not appreciate the gifts that *have* been given to us. If we remember all our gifts—beginning with simple necessities like warmth, water, and food—and consciously feel grateful for them, it is hard to stress out over a lack of abundance at the same time.

Remember: live, love, and laugh. It is the best we can do for all of us—for you and me and all the rest. And as you do your fire ceremonies, be kind to yourself and give the Creator your troubles. When you let go of the negative stuff you've been holding in your heart box, the energy you free up will then be used to keep you healthy. And remember, as Gram would say, to love as unconditionally as you can. That is where true forgiveness comes from, and it begins, of course, with yourself. Loving yourself unconditionally leads to loving other people that way, too, and makes it much easier to view even difficult situations and others with empathy. You might even learn to feel grateful for them. To practice loving instead of tying up your energy in your heart box will save you so much heartache and even physical troubles. How easy is that? It is so simple. Good health and good healing!

All the lessons in this book I learned from my gram. She gave me the job of passing these things on to help the world. I am still running Soaring Eagles Wellness Center and expect to be doing so for some time yet. There are many lessons to teach, and teach I will, in keeping with Gram's wish that this information not be lost.

I hope that you glean what rings true to you from what I've said. And may the rest of your journey here on Mother Earth be a pleasant one. God bless.

—Russell FourEagles

Index

INDEX

Quest Books

encourages open-minded inquiry into
world religions, philosophy, science, and the arts
in order to understand the wisdom of the ages,
respect the unity of all life, and help people explore
individual spiritual self-transformation.

Its publications are generously supported by
The Kern Foundation,
a trust committed to Theosophical education.

Quest Books is the imprint of
the Theosophical Publishing House,
a division of the Theosophical Society in America.
For information about programs, literature,
on-line study, membership benefits, and international centers,
see www.theosophical.org
or call 800-669-1571 or (outside the U.S.) 630-668-1571.

Related Quest titles

Manual for the Peacemaker: An Iroquois Legend to Heal Self and Society, by Jean Houston, with Margaret Rubin

Native Healer, by Medicine Grizzlybear Lake

Path of the Sacred Pipe, by Jay Cleve

The Shaman and the Medicine Wheel, by Evelyn Eaton

Shamanism, by Shirley J. Nicholson

The Vision Keepers, by Doug Alderson

To order books or a complete Quest catalog,
call 800-669-9425 or (outside the U.S.) 630-665-0130.